WIMPIE
the best kept secret

Copyright © 2022 by Wimpie van der Merwe

The right of Wimpie van der Merwe to be identified as the Author of the Work has been asserted in accordance with the Copyright Act 98 of 1978.

All rights reserved. No portion of this book may be reproduced, stored in a retrieval system, or transmitted in any form or by any means, electronic, mechanical, photocopying, recording, or otherwise without the prior permission of the copyright owner.

First Edition February 2022 in paperback

Cover designed by Nobuhle Media

Photographs: All from the authors' own photo library, unless otherwise mentioned.

ISBN: 978-1-991208-60-6

WIMPIE
the best kept secret

Wimpie van der Merwe

For anyone seeking reassurance and comfort in these tremulous times in which we live, this is a book they must read. Ostensibly it is about cycling, and cycling does play a cardinal role in the story. This is as much a spiritual tour de force as it is a gripping saga of one man's resolute determination, steadfastness and conviction underpinned by his amazing faith in God that no hill is too high, no distance too far and no goal too unimaginable that it cannot be attained.

This is an amazing story of self-discovery in that the author recounts with disarming candour his appalling lack of confidence as a child. His suppressed undoubted talent lay in his physical stamina, first discovered in judo and then in his remarkable strength as a cyclist. It is an inspiring story of exceptional leadership as others recognized in him outstanding qualities that he himself found hard to acknowledge. It is a story of endurance as the author sought to go where no man had gone before and in doing so, cracked the Guinness Book of World Records.

It is a story of pain – the pain of defeat and despair as much as the very real pain of achievement and the ability to resurrect oneself from the humiliating jaws of impending disaster to the dizzy heights of victory. It is a story of humility where the author demonstrates incredible grit, guts and determination to succeed against all odds, no matter how devastating the setbacks, no matter how depressing the mental outlook, no matter how discouraging the physical challenges, and he still succeeds, emerging victorious at the end.

It is a story of inspiration where the author is willing to bring you, the reader and the observer on this extraordinary journey with him through these riveting pages, to develop the ability to aspire to the same personalised iconic achievements in your life as he has pioneered in his. And the ultimate secret is… ah, but that would be telling. Read the book for yourself. It will change your life.

Doug McClure
Broadcaster, author, academic

*****

I was blessed by the content of the book. I believe the book will minister to many people. It is a brilliant message that will build great faith in many people.

I believe we have a great product that will certainly impact the Body of Christ and the unsaved that need to experience the Love of God and a faith building message.

The book carries a strong message that shall provoke a deep quest for people to know God more deeply, you skilfully mixed your faith, science and personal experience, the book demonstrated your deep knowledge of the subject matter while building confidence with the reader that you know God in a real way. This validates the content of the book. This is a Kingdom project and we are praying for you.

Dr Tich Tanyanyiwa
Author, success coach, pastor

*****

Hierdie boek is 'n moet. Ek was vasgevang deur die wonderlike gebeure, die engel besoeke en jou vertroue in die Skepper. Elke sportman moet dit op sy boekrak hê, 'wanneer hy dit klaar gelees het'. Elke jong gelowige moet dit lees, want die boek bevat inspirerende boodskappe wat hy nie sommer vanaf 'n preekstoel sal hoor nie.

Dan Oosthuizen

Emeritus pastor

*****

Life is full of adventure and mystery and if you don't believe me, read this book. Wimpie and me had similar experiences but half a world apart. I had it easy, he had it tough. Apartheid made it hard on all world class athletes, but Wimpie persevered to compete at the highest levels. And that is what makes this book so compelling to read. Wimpie is the original "Energizer Bunny" you can't stop him. Not by cycling crashes, muggings or just plain bad luck, God seemingly was right there with Wimpie every step of the way. God has a plan for each and everyone of us and all I can say is God's plan for Wimpie is mighty entertaining to read about. You'll enjoy this book.

Freddy Markham

Former USA Olympian cyclist and world record holder. 22 year career as a top amateur and professional. US National team member 1976–1980. Former Olympic and world championship team member. NCL world Champion, UCI Masters world champion on the road and track. Hundreds of wins on both the track and road. 20 World records in human powered competition including the DuPont Prize in 1986 and the Dempsey Macready hour record in 2006.

*****

CONTENTS

PREFACE	7
1. UNINTENDED CONSEQUENCES	9
2. THE MIRACLES	24
3. ANGELIC VISITATIONS	33
4. THE SCIENTIST	44
5. THE ROADIE	57
6. THE TRACKIE	70
7. THE WORLD RECORDS	88
8. WORLD CHAMPIONSHIPS	106
9. THE RUNNER	123
10. 'VAL & RY' VAN DER MERWE	132
11. THE GIFT – THE QUEEN OF COMEBACK	142
12. FINGERPRINTS	150

PREFACE

MY GRANDFATHER, Alfred Meintjes, was a cyclist in the early 20th Century, but I have no recollection and no history of his exploits, only verbal memories that were passed on by family. These memories died out as the people carrying those memories died. It is a disservice to the following generations that no records were kept and I did not want this to be said about me by the generations that follow me.

When I realised that I had sporting talent I decided to keep every newspaper report possible about my adventures. I believed that these clippings would be some form of reminder for the next generation of what their great, great grandfather did, until one day, my family found out that none of us could recall certain events that were mentioned in the newspaper reports! I had to promise them that I shall put my memories to paper before I forget.

Firstly, this is a work to remind me and my family of the future about events that were important to me. Perhaps it could inspire a grandchild to one day make bigger footprints than me.

Secondly, it is a service to many supporters who want to hear from the horse's mouth about the history that was made and which was not always fully reported on or that has gone lost. Someone once mentioned to me that I was the 'best-kept secret' and that inspired the title.

Thirdly, it is an opportunity to give others insight into things that happened behind the scenes. The press hardly reported the full truth, just what they saw and by hearsay. In many cases, it was to create controversy and sell newspapers.

Fourthly and most importantly, the book is a testimony of God's goodness and grace over a lifetime in someone's sports career. I understand the trappings of fame. I am less interested in my reputation, but more about Godly character. By being transparent I hope others have footprints to follow through this minefield.

1. UNINTENDED CONSEQUENCES

IT IS RUMOURED that the booster rockets of the Space Shuttle's design were based on the width of a horse's butt. These booster rockets are transported from their assembly line to Houston by train. En route, the train has to pass through tunnels. The train and the widest parts of the rockets have to be able to pass through it. The train's width is based on the rut of the railway lines. The distance between the railway lines was based on the rut of the old tram system because they could manufacture the railway lines with the same tooling and equipment. The tram's rut dimensions were based on the grooves the metal bands of the old Roman chariots left in the roads and cobbles. The rut of the chariots was based on the space needed between the two wheels of a Roman chariot to fit two horses to pull it. The result is that the booster rockets of the Shuttle have their design thanks to the width of a Roman horse's butt! This is an example of the law of unintended consequences.

Early on in life bicycles became an integral part of life.

Many things in life may seem to have unintended consequences. From God's perspective, these nudgings were indeed intended, though we still could either follow or resist them. Many events in my life have had seemingly unintended consequences. I have considered if I went to do national service first, would I have met my wife that I married? If not, the children I have would not have been born. Had I not received a tricycle on my third Christmas as a present, but a Dinky toy car, would my interest in cycling still have been ignited? If we stayed closer to school would the need to have bought a commuter bicycle still be there? By riding this bicycle, the love for riding around in the veld and the dirt roads in the neighbourhood was nurtured.

Wimpie always entertaining himself bouncing his stroller.

As a baby I never crawled, I pulled myself along on my butt in my cloth diaper. I always blamed my mom for using me to polish the red stoep with my behind! From my haunches, I was promoted directly to running, skipping the walking phase. I had boundless energy. As a baby, I spent time in the pram and a 'Jolly Jumper'. I amused and kept myself busy by bouncing both up and down all day long.

On this particular day, my pram was parked outside the kitchen window in the morning sun. My mom was busy inside and I was bouncing the pram. A lady, walking in the street, passing our house, saw this pram bouncing up and down by itself in the garden. She just could not contain her curiosity and entered the garden and walked over to where I was. As she peered into the pram to see what was going on, my mom saw her and rushed outside, thinking she could be a baby snatcher! The woman was very apologetic and explained that she has never seen something like this before in her life and had to come and see for herself! I had boundless energy.

Luckily, we had a big garden with lawns, a fruit orchard and ample trees to climb in and expend this energy. I acquired my love for the outdoors at home because to me this was the outdoors. We stayed on an acre plot in Randburg, just north of the Johannesburg city centre where the MNet building currently stands.

> DIE VADERLAND ★ Vrydag 27 Junie 1969 31
>
> DIE LAERSKOOL UNIKA se eerste rugbyspan het vanjaar die derde keer agtereenvolgens Johannesburg se kampioenspan geword deur eergister in die eindwedstryd die Laerskool Theo Wassenaar met 22—3 te klop. Die spannetjie het die seisoen 403 punte aangeteken, terwyl slegs 32 teen hom behaal kon word. Vyf van sy seuns het vir Transvaal se laerskolespan diens gedoen. Hulle is W. van der Merwe, W. Breytenbach, R. Joubert, A. van Wyk en A. Steyn. Op die foto is die kampioenspan op hul rugbyveld afgeneem. AGTER (van links): R. Joubert, J. Mostert, G. Ebersohn, A. van Wyk, A. Steyn. MIDDEL: J. Versveld, W. Breytenbach, R. Potgieter, D. Venter, A. van Vuuren, P. van der Spuy en S. Coetzer. VOOR: H. Muller, W. van der Merwe (kapt.), G. Minnaar en H. Zastro. Die drie onderwysers is van links mnre. S. Coetzer (hoof), T. Winterbach en H. Rossouw.

1969 Transvaal Primary School champions – Unika Primary School.

Our home was a typical suburban home for the time. At 6 years of age, my father upgraded the house to have an indoor toilet. If ever you needed to go, whether in the dark, freezing winter night or the rain, you had to go out to the outhouse in the middle of the garden where the pump house and room for the wood storage were. At night, with a horse-drawn carriage, men removed the sewage pots. One night one was removed from under me, whilst still on the toilet. These made indelible impressions on a young child's mind.

Wood storage was necessary to make a fire in the copper geyser in the bathroom before anyone could have warm water. As a result, everyone used the same water when we had to bathe. I bathed last and could stay in the longest, many times falling asleep in the water.

I went to a large primary school, Unika, in Robindale. I enjoyed school, especially the rugby and games played before school and during breaks. As children, we tried to be at school the earliest possible, because that gives you bragging rights and the best skating surfaces on the rugby field in the morning frost, before anyone else has skated the frost off the grass.

My first excelling at sport came with Rugby when I was chosen as captain for the first team. We became the southern Transvaal champions for 1969. I was selected to play loose forward for the Transvaal schools' team. We played a raiser game on Ellispark before the main match. I remember the feeling of playing before thousands of cheering people. The distances between the posts were double the distance than on our home field! You had to pack in a lunch pack just to make it between the goal lines. It was the times you knew the names of each player of the Transvaal and Springbok rugby teams. There was no TV, just your ear glued to the radio, listening to Gerhard Viviers, the commentator, and having the game play out before your mind's eye.

I finished primary school and was enrolled in Randburg High School, a newly built school not too far from us. The clothes were bought and ready to go when I received a call from my mom from work the day before the school year started, saying that my parents were enrolling me in Linden High School. I was to go and swop the clothes at the store for those of Linden. Unintended consequences? What would have happened with my life had I not changed schools? I believe God was nudging, knowing where He was going with my life in the future.

I liked high school, especially the outdoor activities. The curriculum was not really of consequence. I was an active Voortrekker, already from standard 1. I met my best friends through Voortrekkers, people who I still have the greatest respect for today.

I was twice Victor Ludorum in athletics (junior and senior) and the athletics captain in 1974. I did not really excel in anything, but could do everything and win most of my track and field events, but could not become a representative of the provincial athletics team.

I played Rugby and for the first team. My Rugby heroes all became broken physically and I decided that I would not want to end up like them, with knee and back problems. I left the sport after school for this reason.

As a teenager, I lacked confidence. This equalled the lack of confidence I had with the opposite sex. Everyone had a girlfriend of some sort and I did not. My interest would just be at looking and never having the confidence to speak to the one I was admiring. This lack of confidence got me connected to Judo. A circular was sent around at school, inviting any person who has a lack of confidence to come for a free session at the Dojo across the street from the school. The part that caught my interest was where it mentioned the lack of confidence in speaking in front of the class.

If I look back where my confidence took a severe beating as a child it was the pressure placed on the children to participate in Eisteddfod, a talent competition in reciting and singing. Most children were encouraged to participate and then had to compete in front of a hall full of people. I was terrified. I felt humiliated when I forgot my words. The certificate that you received, gold, silver or green, indicated your worth. I wanted to excel, but in areas I was good in and not being forced to excel in areas which I had no interest in. Subtle peer pressure was used to force a square peg into a round hole. This caused damage. Physical activities were my forte.

I started Judo at the age of 14. My instructor was Joe Knoester, Dutch in origin, who had a knack for kids. He called me 'Kleintje'. The benefit of his tutoring for me was more in the mentoring than in the art of Judo.

I was bullied at school. Before school, there were these playground thugs who always intimidated me. Since my mom warned me that I may not become involved in school fights I knew even before the facts were known I would first get a hiding and then I shall be given an ear. This made me the bullies' punching bag. I always had to avoid the scuffles, but in place had to endure the verbal abuse. I refused to use my bullies' dictionary either.

All the bullying changed when I became skilful in Judo, not because I could defend myself, but because I had the confidence that I knew I could fight and did not need to prove it. This confidence scared them more than anything else. This did not stop their verbal abuse, but they were kept at bay.

Up to 15 years old only my father had shaved my head. The style was a crew cut, short back, side and top, the simplest haircut that could be given. However, for a young teenager, growing up in the times of the hippies where long hair was the custom, a crew cut was not sexy or esteemed. The only way you could see the difference between the sexes then was by following the person to the toilet to see which door it entered in. The girls seemingly liked the guys with longer hair. My crew cut might have been popular with the school teachers –

Trajan Grobler, Jan Malan, Sidney Zeeman and Wimpie van der Merwe rode for Springbok Radio Christmas Fund from Walvisbay to Johannesburg in 1974.

one less child to discipline for long hair – but for my confidence, it had zero value. Judo was thus an extremely powerful tool to build my self-image.

I eventually became the provincial junior champion in my weight division and represented Transvaal who won the SA championship team competition in 1974. Had I continued, I believe I could have become a Springbok too.

Cadets were part of the school curriculum and practised as a school activity. I could honestly say that the one activity that had the greatest imprint on my development was the participation in the special drill platoon. This platoon was in demand to show off the skills of choreographed drilling. It had a national championship of which Linden became national champions in 1973 and runner-up in 1974. The skills of discipline, teamwork, coordination and hard work were ingrained.

As a Voortrekker, I acquired a love for the outdoors. Outdoor life and acquiring survival skills were popular. SA was becoming a tense place. We started hearing of clashes on our borders and terrorist attacks becoming more frequent. These skills were seen as needed. Voortrekkers prepared people more psychologically for the expected and unexpected than those who were not part of it. In the military, these were the young men who already had a head start.

It is in the Voortrekkers where my cycling started. One of our Voortrekker team members' mom, was Joey de Koker. She was one of the known voices in the radio soapies and radio dramas of the time. She worked at Springbok Radio at the SABC. Every year Springbok Radio had a Christmas money drive for the Springbok Radio Christmas Fund. On air, people could challenge one another to match or to better their pledged donation. On this particular day the fuel company, Mobil, challenged anyone who could travel cheaper than with their fuel. They would pay the difference. Trajan Grobler, Joey's son, immediately responded and accepted the challenge. We shall ride from Johannesburg to Cape Town by bicycle on the reverse route of the inaugural Rapport Tour, which was held for the first time that year (1973) from Cape Town to Johannesburg.

Springbok Radio staff with Sidney Zeeman, Wimpie van der Merwe and Trajan Grobler before commencing their ride from Johannesburg to Cape Town in 1973.

DRIE van die vier skoolseuns wat pas matriek afgelê het en Saterdag 'n rit van byna 2 700 km aanpak om reklame te maak vir die Voortrekkers. Hulle is van links Sidney Zeeman, Wimpie van der Merwe en Jan Malan.

Vier seuns swoeg Namib deur vir geld

VIER jong kêrels wat pas die matriekeksamen afgelê het, spring Saterdag op hul ysterperde weg uit Swakopmund in Suidwes. Hulle gaan tot in Johannesburg trap — om vir die Voortrekkers reklame te maak.

Die lang, warm pad sal vir hulle gaan oor die Namib-woestyn tot op Windhoek en van daar met die grootpad langs.

Die vier was almal leerlinge van die Hoërskool Linden in Johannesburg.

Hulle is Jan Malan — hy was vanjaar Linden se hoofseun — Wimpie van der Merwe, Sidney Zeeman en Trajan Grobler.

Dis nie die eerste keer dat die kêrels die lang pad vat nie. Verlede jaar het hulle van Johannesburg na Kaapstad gery. Toe het hulle die tog aangepak om geld in te samel vir Springbokradio se Kersfonds. Hulle het meer as R1 000 ingesamel.

'n Petrolmaatskappy het destyds 'n groot bydrae gelewer om die geld in te samel. Die maatskappy het 'n uitdaging gerig aan enigiemand om goedkoper te ry as met hulle soort brandstof. Die seuns het die antwoord gehad — ysterperde! En die petrolmense moes opdok.

Hoogste rang

Vanjaar is dit die Voortrekkers wat munt slaan uit die kêrels se energie. Drie van die vier het vanjaar die hoogste rang vir Voortrekkers bereik — hulle is Presidentsverkenners. Die Voortrekkers borg dan ook gedeeltelik vanjaar se poging. Die fietsryers het net die nodigste by hulle. Om die geldjies te rek, sal hulle dalk 'n paar keer moet gebruik maak van die Staatspresident se gasvryheid vir slaapplek — polisieselle.

Jan Malan is die seun van dr. Jannie Malan, NG predikant van Aasvoëlkop, en hy het 'n brief by pa gekry. Die brief stel die vier bekend aan predikante langs die pad en dis seker dat hulle dáár ook vriendelik ontvang sal word.

Op Saterdag, 19 Desember, kom hulle in Johannesburg aan, van waar hulle gister per trein na Swakopmund vertrek het.

That morning Trajan arrived at school and informed Sidney Zeeman and me that we are riding 1,400 km to Cape Town in December by bicycle. We were teased by the naysayers and the doubting Thomases. I only had a primitive school commuting bike. I had to empty my Post Office savings account and buy myself a light blue Carlton racer, fully equipped with cotter pins and clincher tyres for the whopping price of just under R30. On the recommendation of the bike store, I bought cycling shorts too. We did this adventure in about 13 days and returned by train.

We were received in the Springbok Radio studio in Seapoint, Cape Town and there we committed ourselves for the next adventure publicly, Walvis Bay to Johannesburg. Trajan Grobler moved down to Durban with his family and finished his schooling there. Jan Malan joined us as the fourth rider for the next trip.

Since we completed our mission from Johannesburg to Cape Town successfully, we were not laughing stock at school anymore but objects of admiration. Our school headmaster was the author, Cor Dirks, who wrote the 'Die Uile' series. Our trip inspired him to write a story in 1973 about this and incorporate it into his numerous lists of Die Uile books, 'Die Uile in die Wapad'.

In 1974 we wrote our matric exams and directly after that boarded the train to Swakopmund. We were under the impression that when passing through the Namib desert we shall be struck by heat, especially crossing it in the middle of summer. It became so cold that we had to pull off the road and shelter against one another in a stormwater pipe under the road.

We were passing through very harsh terrain, crossing two deserts, the Namib and Kalahari. In most cases, the water we left with in the morning was the only water we had for the day. We carried 3 one-pint bottles of water on the bike, two on the handlebar and one on the frame. Your luggage was in a saddlebag and a sling-on bag, across your shoulder and back. We had a minimalist approach concerning luggage. Our clothing was just our civvies and the day's cycling gear. The latter you wash when you arrive at your place to stay for the night, whilst wearing the others.

We enjoyed every moment of this style of touring and looking back, this was the correct way for me to start cycling. I discovered the enjoyment aspect of cycling first. I had something to recall whenever I had a very competitive and strenuous time when the enjoyment of cycling was lost. Riding just for enjoyment would eventually become the foundation for my future health and longevity in cycling.

Jan Malan and I were both selected as head boy and deputy head boy, respectively and thus served in leadership. Various leadership positions I served in at school and sport did not assure me the confidence and acceptance I needed as a person. It was just 'a nice to have'.

The school recognised my leadership skills and proficiency in sport and went all out to recruit me for the education profession. I was even called into the headmaster's office where the inspector of education could meet me and assure me that it would be the right decision.

I was enrolled at Potch University for a Physical Education degree with a full bursary. This did not stick with my parents, because at the time teachers did not make enough money. On the other hand, I was looking for a challenge, typically the person I am. At the last moment, I decided to enrol for a law degree at the Rand Afrikaans University (RAU), now University of Johannesburg. I could not find accommodation at that late point in time at the University of Stellenbosch, my first choice. Again, the effect of unintended consequences came into action. Had I gone to Potch or Stellenbosch I would never have met my wife and would possibly not have started a cycling career.

In 1975, at the age of 17, I enrolled for B.Proc at RAU. RAU was 4 years old by then and it was the first year that the new campus in Aucklandpark was used. Though my home was 10 km from campus I stayed on campus in the hostel, Afslaan.

In those years RAG was within the first quarter of the year. The hostels competed for a trophy, the 'Baron Gawie' trophy. The competition was based on accumulating points, based on the level of media exposure you can generate for either hostel or university. National newspapers would carry more weight than news only in a local newspaper. It was a couple of months before TV was launched in SA. As part of my contribution to the RAG effort, I broke the world cycling record Springbok Dries Oberholzer set a short while before me, bettering it from 111 to 120 hours of non-stop cycling.

The record garnered media attention in all the local newspapers and for two weeks everybody on campus got to know who I was. I was flattered. Then one of the most crucial things in my life happened. After two weeks nobody was talking about this anymore. Life moved on. The recognition I was craving was deflating like a balloon. I had no intention of repeating something like this.

I continued to experience this vacuum within me increasingly that needed filling. It was a search and desire to give meaning to my life. Whatever I did as a way to gain recognition and acceptance with people was like drinking saltwater. It never quenched my thirst. People looking in from the outside would say I was a well-behaved boy, well mannered, 'a real Christian'. However, they did not know how empty I really was and how much I was searching for meaning. I did not follow the route of drinking and partying.

I was doing the 'right things', but the 'right things' were not fulfilling. I was linked into the local Christian student community. By the middle of my first year, I already attended and participated in 11 evangelistic training courses. This is where you are taught how to lead someone into a relationship with Jesus, how to address objections, etc. Looking back this was keeping me from filling the vacuum I was experiencing in my life.

When you are vaccinated, a little bit of the virus is injected into you, activating your immune system to fight the virus by forming antibodies. This way your body will never be affected by the virus when it comes in contact with you, it will be prepared to reject it. My spiritual body was being vaccinated by the courses I was doing. If the Gospel was the virus, I was being prepared to reject it because I had all the prepared answers to the questions asked. I could tick off all the blocks for the right answers, but actually, I have not yet entered into a relationship with Jesus. Mentally I was agreeing to every truth of the Gospel, but I was just as saved as a rock dropped into the ocean.

For a birthday present my roommate in Afslaan, Ferdinand van Niekerk and his then-girlfriend, gave me a book of the paraphrase of the letters of Paul, written by Helen Steiner Rice. I decided to stay in the hostel during the September holidays and use it for studies and reading. I started reading this book. Where I was inoculated by the form and sound of the text in the Bible that I usually read, I got the same message just in a different way. It was like being exposed to a variant of the virus, against which the previous vaccination did not work.

For the first time, the realization was that I was asking the wrong question. It should not be, what must I do to fill the vacuum in my life? It should rather be: Who should fill it? This was the beginning of my life of meaning and the end of searching for ways to give life meaning. The searching was over. There was peace. I could look myself in the mirror and know God accepted me, with my pimples and imperfections. I did not need to do any panel beating to make myself acceptable to Him. I could leave that to Him. From now on I was a work in progress.

With this event in my life, changes came. I received a calling from God for the ministry. I decided to complete my first year of B.Proc so that at least I cannot be accused of backing out for an easier course because the one I enrolled for was too difficult. I knew my choice for the ministry was going to meet resistance from my parents and that I cannot rely on their financial assistance for the seven-year theological degree. To pay for this I started doing security work part-time at night, whilst at RAU.

Another thing that happened was an immediate end in the desire to do any sport. Sport, up to that point was a way to acquire recognition and give meaning to a meaningless existence. My life now had meaning and sport was unnecessary. I experienced peace and joy. During my first year of theological studies, my path crossed with Christa Holtzhausen, my eventual wife. I am grateful for this unintended consequence of changing from Potch to RAU.

For me to complete my studies at Stellenbosch, my first choice of place of study, I had to make my move then. I had to start my second year of studies at the university where I wanted to eventually graduate. I successfully applied to Stellenbosch and was accepted. My school friend, Gysbert Wessels, was already in Stellenbosch. By now I was not interested in cycling anymore. I sold my bike to him for commuting.

As I was daily walking back from class at Stellenbosch, I passed a tree on the sidewalk of Victoria Street where many cyclists were meeting daily. Each day at five o'clock these guys were there leaving on their training rides. Every time I walked past them my heart beat faster and I felt the excitement rise in me.

God then gave me the release to stop and chat bicycles with them. He trusted me with doing sport again. The motive would be pure this time. I wanted to ride with them. They talked about an upcoming race, a tour that would be held in the April holidays, going from Stellenbosch to Viljoenskroon. There would be three teams of four men each and you have to be selected to participate in the 'Tour de Maties'. By now my heart was pumping.

I approached Gysbert and asked if I could borrow the bike, I sold him, for a while? This led me to become involved in cycling again, participating in the 1977 Tour de Maties, coming second overall and first in the points classification. I started racing on the Western Province calendar but had no tactical skills. I worked the hardest of all but was never rewarded with a podium for this until much later.

Whilst staying in Helshoogte hostel on campus, my next-door neighbour was Bobby McGee, the eventual Olympic trainer of SA's first gold medallist in the marathon in the Olympic Games in Atlanta, Matthew Thugwane. He was busy with his Honours degree in Physical Education. He stated that they were looking for guinea pigs to test in the Phys Ed lab. They were busy with VO2 max testing of people and from there onwards to make predictions in which sports they would excel. They already had a physical profile of several Springbok and international sportsmen and this could help me as I was feeling like a Jack of all trades, but master of none. I rise to the provincial level and then get stuck. It might be due to the selection of my sports.

I tested for a week long. The result: canoeing and cycling. I was of international calibre in both. I told Bobby I knew nothing about rowing, but I have ridden a bicycle. I shall rather pursue the latter. A few months later he was proven right when I was selected for my first Rapport Tour in 1977 to ride with Alan van Heerden, Eddie King, Raymond Hogg and Jan van der Berg in the Solly Kramer team.

My international cycling career eventually spanned a couple of decades, riding international tours locally and overseas, competing in several tests on the track against international teams for the Springboks and Federation team. I participated in 9 Rapport Tours, 'stretched my legs' in world record attempts and world championships, 'stretched the mind' in ultra-endurance events like Everesting and Audaxes. I explored the limits of speed and endurance. I had my share of physical and mental agony. I had the high and lows of victories and defeat.

The 1977 Solly Kramers Rapport Tour team.

I know what it means to be lifted and venerated and to be humiliated and trodden down by the same.

I have had enough 'me time' to do introspection and question what I do. I have acquired enough distance in time from the events I participated in to gain perspective to see where they have added value to people or a country or whether these events left a destructive legacy.

As part of my introspection, I try to learn from myself as if I am someone else. I tried to determine WHY do I do what I do? For my first world record, I could say, for the recognition of people, but that was removed as a motivational force the moment I received acceptance with God. I found it difficult in formulating this WHY. What is the reason why I go through the rigours of training, the daily discipline of sweating and suffering, swimming upstream and not floating downstream, not being a couch potato, etc?

The reason why I am sure most people will not be able to verbalise it is that the WHY of life is a limbic activity. In layman's terms it means, the WHY is formulated in the part of the brain where emotions are formed, not where words and speech are formulated. Therefore, your WHY will feel right on an emotional level. It will resonate with your spirit man and not necessarily with your reason. People try to express their WHY by explaining WHAT they do and HOW they do things.

Doing a 10,000m Everest on Franschhoek pass, one of more than a dozen sole attempts.

Let me take you through my journey how I discovered my WHY. I discovered it quite late in my sporting career. I was doing something right. Yes, there were times I failed, but I will eventually be remembered for the times I succeeded. I was curious to find out what has been the common factor in all my accomplishments? What is it that kept me going when I wanted to quit?

I found out that there are two participants in the internal conversation in me, 'Me' and 'Myself'. They are always engaged in a conversation. The one wants to take the easy way out and the other wants to go on when the going gets tough. When I look at the events that I failed in, in my opinion, I can recall the conversation that was going on and who won the argument, 'Me' or 'Myself'. I can also recall the conversations I had when I succeeded.

I started looking for a common topic, especially when 'Me' and 'Myself' started arguing about why am I doing it? 'Myself' can come up with an argument, 'nobody knows you are doing this event and nobody shall know if you quit'. These are especially true when I do Everesting, all on my own, riding the height of Everest (8,848 m) with no one as support present. 'Me' has to counter why there shall be no quitting today. I found out that the same reasons for not quitting are the same as years ago during world championships and world record attempts.

To find my WHY I had to 'percolate' these internal conversations until just the dry powder lay on the bottom of the pot, reduced to just one or two main reasons I had as motivation to keep going and not quitting.

You need to understand, the WHY is not a big deal when you are just before the victory line or seconds away from a world record. The greatest demand for your WHY is when you have to get up in the dark, when it is cold, rainy and you are still sleepy, to overcome the comfort of Mr P Low and Mrs Du Vet. This is when you will have to draw on your WHY. In the easy times especially, you will have to draw on your WHY. Comfort is a bigger enemy of WHY than discomfort. Comfort is like a tranquillizer. You let go of your WHY little bit by little bit. You become fatter little bit by little bit. You become lazy, little bit by little bit. The frog is boiled live in the pot and because it happens in increments, he does not jump out. Had you thrown him in the same water he would have leapt out immediately.

Wake-up calls in life, the health, financial or other kinds of crises, act as very good motivators to get someone into action. That is the adrenalin injection which gets the heart pumping again. Your WHY has to overcome the lullaby song of the ease of inaction and procrastination, the temptation of taking the easy way out, following the way of least resistance, floating downstream like a dead fish.

I discovered my WHY by doing introspection and questioned my motives to see whether they were relevant and applicable in previous testing times. My WHY cannot become your WHY, because a WHY cannot be given, it has to be discovered and the glove fits my 6 fingered hand. Here is why I do what I do. This is the core of Wimpie van der Merwe at the high and the low. The result of this WHY can be measured by my sports accomplishments over decades.

> *'I continuously strive to be the best I can be and live an abundant life, a life of contentment, a life of no regrets. I challenge man-made and perceived limits. I challenge the status quo and write my own history.'*

By being true to my WHY throughout my sporting career I was able to become a person of consequence. What were initially unintended consequences became intentional. By living a purposeful life, I could achieve what only a few other cyclists achieved. This can be true for anyone, but then you have to first overcome the very low hurdles of being able to motivate yourself in the small things like training daily, disciplining your eating habits, managing your speech, etc. Success lies in the mind. Without success habits, there will be no success.

2. THE MIRACLES

IF YOU SIT down and contemplate what the Good News, the Gospel of Jesus, is, you can say a couple of things about what it is and what it isn't. Some consider the Gospel to be the message about the goodness of God, contained in a book, called the Bible, but for the Muslims, the Koran is the same. It is a book with information on the perceived goodness of their god, Allah. Thus, information about the goodness of God is not the uniqueness of the Gospel. Preaching and sharing the goodness of God is only part of the answer.

The uniqueness, however, lies in the demonstration of power. This is what convinces people about God and His goodness. The information about the goodness of God has to be backed up with evidence: signs, wonders and miracles. The Gospel of Jesus is NOT powerless. It does the miraculous. It is super-natural, above, more than the natural. The full Gospel is not just preaching or the teaching of doctrine, but demonstrating the power of God. The world wants to see and experience power. God's power offers more than the power of the world or what the enemy can offer.

Jesus performed reconstructive miracles in my body. This is the manifesting proof of His goodness and power. The demonstrated power of God is more convincing than talking and witnessing about God. The following is my experience of the powerful acts of God in my life. Some were sought, some not. God acted through me when I was weak and dependent on Him, using me as a platform to demonstrate His power.

These miracles do not indicate anything special about me, but rather how great a God we have. Possibly I have childlike faith, expecting God to be able to do this because He says He is in the miracle doing business. He demonstrates his power and love to those with an expectant heart and to those who do not deserve it.

DISLOCATED SHOULDER
For 34 years I suffered from a dislocating shoulder due to being swung by the arm in a primary school rugby game. Whenever I lifted my arm above my head and tilted it backwards it popped out. There were certain movements I could never do due to the possibility of having a recurrence. This carried on for 34 years.

In a church service our pastor, faithful to the voice and unction of the Holy Spirit, said that there was someone in the service with a shoulder injury. I responded. It was simple. He prayed, laid his hands on me and I was healed instantly. I have not suffered any recurrence ever since.

RUNNING INJURIES

In 2000 I started running long distances for the first time and got myself proper running shoes. However, initially, my shoes and I were not good friends. The side of the shoes chafed me on the outside of the ankle as if my feet were sticking in too deep into the shoe or the side of the shoes being too high and too rigid. This chafing went on for a couple of weeks. It caused so much damage, no matter how I tried to cover and pad the wound. I had a hole of about 1.5 x 1.5 cm in circumference that went through the skin and was exposing muscle and bone. It was excruciating to put any shoes on and unthinkable to run, but I had to because I was preparing for the Two Oceans and Comrades marathons.

As I was going out for a training run this particular day and reaching the corner of the street where I lived, it suddenly dawned on me that I shall have what I tolerate. I have been tolerating the injury and God gives me the authority to speak healing over the injury. I stopped, bent down, put my hand on the hole and commanded it in the name of Jesus to be healed. In front of my eyes, the gap closed. I did not act surprised. I expected it. I placed a demand on God's power and He acted.

In about 2001, on another run, during a typical wet, wintry day, I was running on the slope of the Helderberg mountain. As I was running in the forest the pine needles covered the ground like a thick soft carpet. It was an enjoyable run. At a point, as I was going downhill, on a slope, covered with this slippery carpet of pine needles, my feet slipped from under me and I fell onto this soft bed. What I did not notice was the branch under the carpet of needles and as I hit the deck a sharp branch pierced the inside of my lower arm. As I pulled the stick out it left a deep gash more than 2 cm wide and as deep. At that instant, I could see the artery and the wound that was filled with debris and mud.

As I clamped my hand over the wound, I had to take control of the inner conversation. I knew I served a great God. He has never failed me before. I asked myself what did He require of me in that situation? The first was: to be thankful in every and all situations. I loudly declared to God that I am thankful for what occurred. He did not require that I understand why it happened, just to be grateful and trust Him fully. It took faith to declare that because I did not need this at that point in my life. As a family, we had a severe cash flow situation and medical expenses were a no-no.

As I walked home the last couple of kilometres, I thanked God over and over. At home, I took my hand off the wound for the first time. No hole, it was fully healed and restored. God honoured and reacted to my faith and not my need.

INJURIES DUE TO AN ASSAULT

Cycling has some risks of which personal safety is one. I stay in Strand, in the Western Cape. Over the first few days of January, the area is very much still in a festive atmosphere where people stay up till late and party on the beach through the night.

It was the 2nd of January, at first light, when I rode along the beach road on my way to join my training group. Three men suddenly attacked me as I passed them. One knocked me off my bicycle and in the process of falling, I fractured my lower leg (fibula), which I did not immediately realise. As I came upright one hit me with a bottle over the head, smashing my cycling helmet. The third stormed at me with a knife with about a 30 cm blade, trying to stab me. They were not trying to rob me but to do me serious bodily harm. I used my bicycle as a shield between me and my attackers. They encircled me.

My broken leg prevented me from using it. I could only pivot on the functional one. In the ensuing battle, the one behind me grabbed the back wheel of my bicycle and as he jerked it to rip it out of my hands, he dislocated my shoulder. By then a motorist stopped and pepper-sprayed them. I was taken in the boot of a car to the hospital since no ambulances were responding to our calls.

The shoulder was put back under anaesthetics and the X-rays indicated a spiral fracture of the lower limb, my fibula. Before any treatment could commence God healed my leg miraculously. I was kept overnight and the next morning I was out on my normal training ride with no pain of any kind!

FRACTURED ARM & INJURED NECK
As I sometimes cycle in extreme weather I dehydrate regularly. This affects blood pressure by lowering it, due to decreased blood plasma levels. On this particular day, I had a long ride. I dehydrated and later that evening as I got up from bed and started walking to the exit of the room, I passed out, falling backwards, hitting my head and neck against furniture and in the process breaking my left upper arm.

As I came by, I tried to get up by pressing with my left arm onto the ground. All I could feel was the grating of bone against bone as the fracture moved. I could not get up. I realised my predicament. My wife, Christa, in a wheelchair, could not get me up either. I told her to phone an ambulance and to phone friends because I shall have to be admitted to hospital and

I was attacked whilst cycling which left me with a broken leg and dislocated shoulder. God healed the leg fracture within hours. One attacker hit me with a beer bottle over the head and used the shattered bottle stub to stab me.

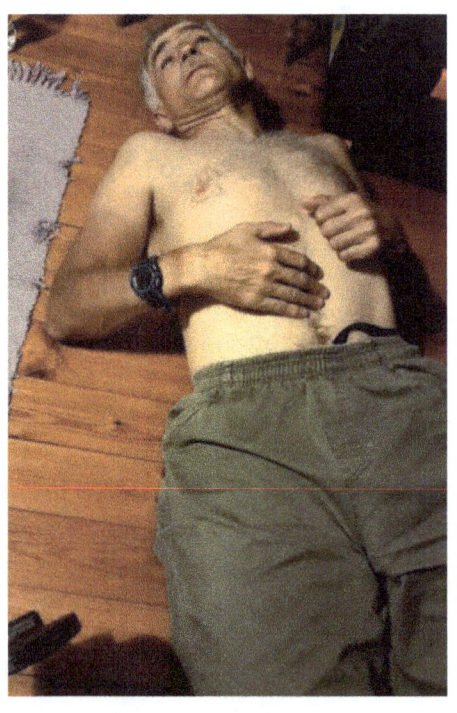

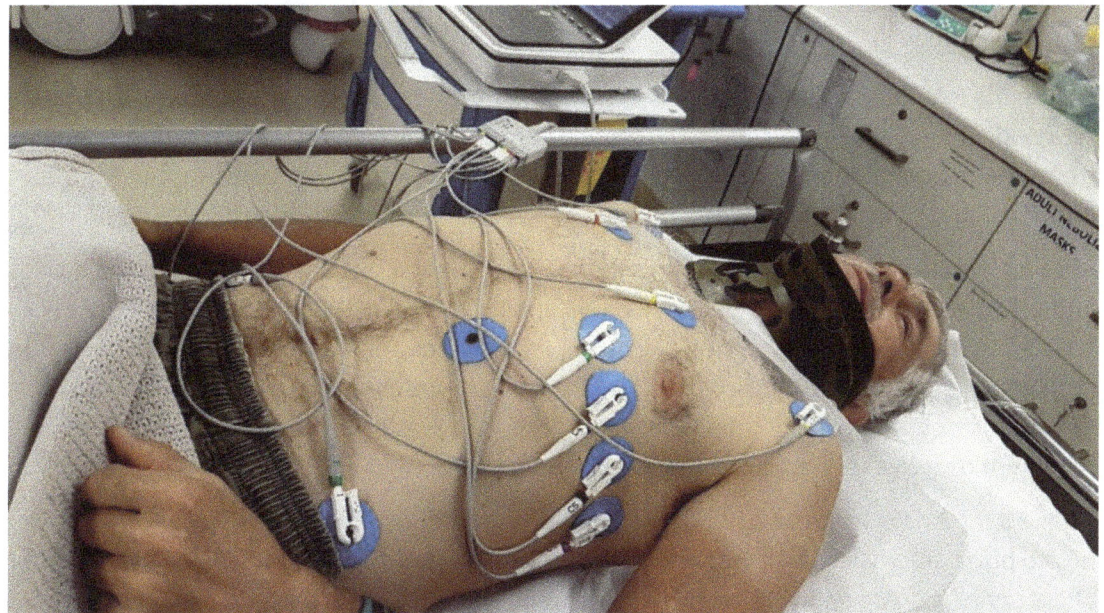

I passed out when I stood up, was taken to hospital and there God did a reconstructive miracle at Radiology when He healed my broken left arm and injured neck. X-rays proved the miracle.

she, as a handicapped person, taken care of in my absence.

When my friends arrived, we prayed for the injuries, my spine and arm, to recover. The paramedics confirmed the fracture and tied my arm to my side and put a neck brace on. I was transported to casualties at the local hospital. I was readied for X-rays. Every time the medical staff handled me, I was in terrible pain, even though I already received my 'happy juice'.

As they pushed me into X-rays and I was lying there on my own, the miracle occurred. My pain disappeared instantaneously. I moved my arm and it was normal. I must admit, I felt God was making a fool out of me. Could He not have waited till the proof was there on X-ray before He healed me? The people would now think I was crying, 'Wolf, Wolf!' I then asked God, if he can do this for my arm, why not for my spine too? The Holy Spirit instructed me to take the brace off to test the neck. At that moment, as I was removing the brace the staff walked in. They dived onto me as if into a loose scrum in a Rugby match to prevent me from doing this.

When they later left, I removed it. The neck was perfect. I felt extremely awkward. I knew it was a miracle, but how do I explain this to a Medical Aid, when claiming for the incident? Luckily the doctor was sympathetic and suggested we X-ray the injured parts in any case and keep me overnight. Here is the interesting part. The X-ray indicated a healed fracture. I have never before broken this arm and the only explanation was that of a reconstructive miracle. X-rays of the neck and spine proved that everything was as it should be.

The next morning, I was released and I went for my daily training ride.

FRACTURED SPINE 1

In 2013 my wife spent months in hospital due to a hospital bug that she attracted there. She nearly lost her life in the process. Eventually, after nearly 3 months in hospital, she was released. The next day I decided to become a gardener and to remove some dead branches from a palm tree on the property, an event which put me into hospital with serious injuries. I fell off the top rung of a 5 m ladder. My wife and I exchanged places of residence seamlessly!

I came down headfirst on brick paving, snapping my back, crushing my elbow, breaking ribs and my foot. My injuries were such that the specialists had to perform various operations over a couple of days. I had 3 spinal compression fractures. My elbow was shattered in multiple fragments and the bones in my foot had to be wired together. The broken ribs were the most painful of them all. The best prognosis was that I would be in hospital for a minimum of 3 weeks and wear a brace for 3-6 months.

After about 3 days I started having breathing problems. I could not breathe automatically. I had to purposefully inhale. It was diagnosed as a torn diaphragm, causing an air leak into the chest cavity, gaining pressure and then collapsing the lungs. The surgeon placed me on the theatre roll for surgery to find the tear. From diagnosis to surgery God healed the tear. The surgeon could not find it and my oxygen saturation returned to normal.

To make a long story short, I walked out on day 7 and drove home in my car, which the doctors said would not be possible. I got on my bicycle and resumed my training.

When I had my follow-up visit with the doctor who operated on my elbow, he found the elbow attached incorrectly and I could only extend my elbow halfway. Another operation would have to be done to remove bone to extend the range of motion. God decided differently. A Christian lady laid hands on the elbow and God moved bones there and then, another reconstructive miracle. Today I have a fully functional elbow.

FRACTURED SPINE 2

Six months after falling out of the tree I went out for a training ride and as I was returning home, on the steep downhill at the Lord Charles Hotel in Somerset West, a car and I collided when the driver of the car turned in front of me when I passed through the intersection at speed.

The ambulance staff later told me that my injuries looked like someone who was not going to make it. I had traumatic head and neck injuries. My head burst open like a watermelon. I needed 52 stitches to put Humpty Dumpty together again. I broke my back in 6 places. I fractured my pelvis and broke ribs which punctured my lung. I spent time in ICU on a ventilator. My left arm was half paralysed due to nerve damage in my neck and the muscles atrophied noticeably within days. By now I knew my God and that 'normal' things don't occur when I am injured. I could be bold and daring and place a demand on the supernatural.

I asked the physio in ICU, who was there to assist with my ventilation if he would entrust me with the ventilator? As he knew me, he agreed. I then pumped up my chest cavity with

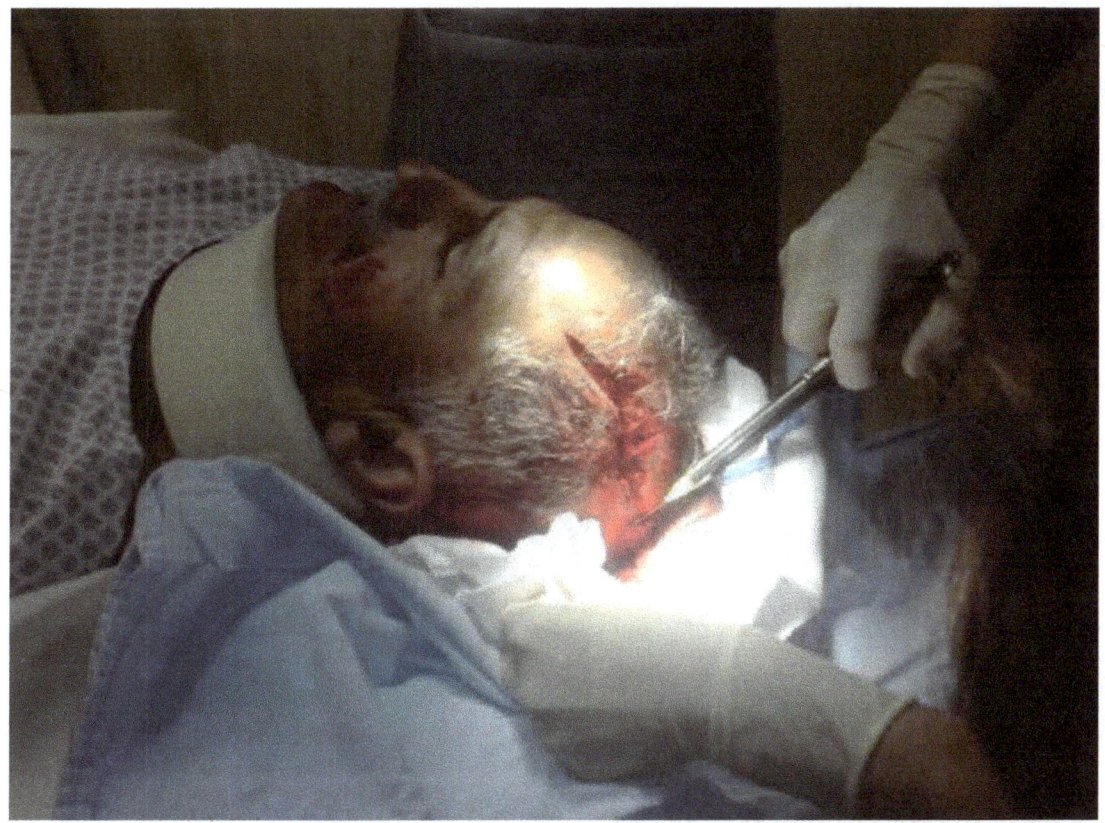

Severe head lacerations, skull, back, pelvis and multiple rib fractures were miraculously healed within 6 days.

the ventilator through my mouth. The overlapping ribs popped back into position and this prevented them from perforating the lungs any further. I was then released from ICU.

With my fractured back and pelvis, I could not walk and had to re-educate my body to do so again. At night when the other patients were sleeping, I was painfully moving with my two crutches along the corridors telling my legs what to do. I was unwilling to accept a catastrophic outcome. By God's grace, I landed with a neuro and orthopaedic surgeon who understood my level of faith and commitment to a positive outcome. I would not accept defeat and I had too much faith in God to allow that.

Here is the miracle. Six days after being admitted with life-threatening injuries from a fractured skull, spine and pelvis, to collapsed lungs, I walked out of the hospital, drove home in my car and started training. The plastic surgeon later told me that when he removes staples and stitches from patients' heads, after 10 days, it is normally from scabs. Mine was near perfect skin.

When the neuro-surgeon released me from the hospital he prescribed pain medication for my neck injury and scheduled an invasive and very delicate surgery which had a 50-50 chance of success. The purpose was to relieve the nerve that was passing through a vertebra and was trapped due to the accident. When I offered my script to the pharmacist to collect my pain medication she asked me whether I know what I have been prescribed? As I did not know, she explained that the medication I was placed on was given only to terminally ill patients who they did not care whether they became addicted or not. She phoned the surgeon in theatre to confirm that he actually prescribed the drugs. He confirmed and explained that the pain I experience can only be addressed by the ones prescribed. The pharmacist then gave me only a week's prescription to do what she could to protect me from becoming addicted.

Realizing the seriousness of my condition and the excruciating pain I was constantly in I again approached the lady who previously laid hands on me for my elbow injury. She laid hands on my neck and instantly the pain was gone and all discomfort. My operation was scheduled

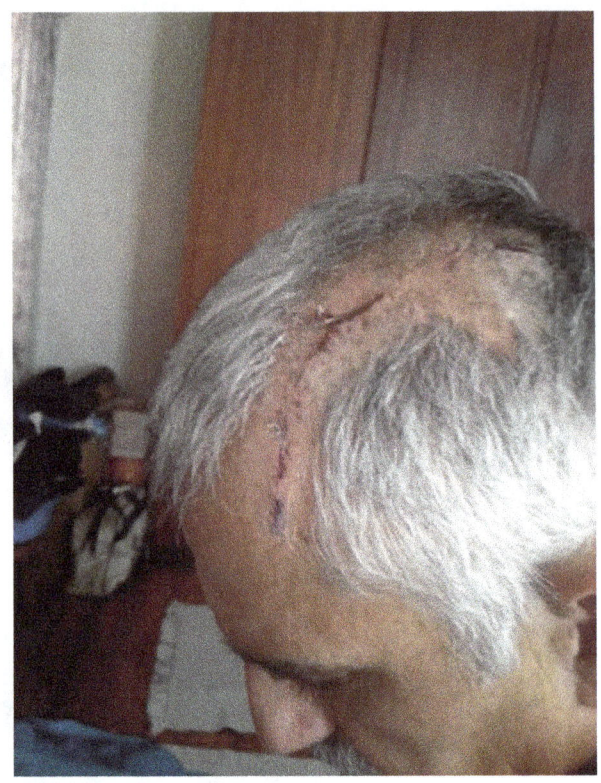

Skull fracture + Head wound healed

and I went to see the neuro-surgeon for a follow-up visit where I informed him that I am cancelling the operation. His question to me was whether I was afraid of it? Since he knew the level of pain that accompanies such an injury and me not asking for a script renewal, he realized that my healing was genuine. His question in disbelief was, 'Where would the bone disappear to?' For me to have what I experienced could only be described as a reconstructive miracle performed by God.

OLYMPIC GAMES

Though this miracle is not a healing miracle it is still a miracle of note where God proved his faithfulness and power. I led a SCAS ministry team to the 1992 Barcelona Olympic Games. Our purpose was to reach out to the Olympians and their helpers at the Games. The best place for us to do that was in the Olympic village. The Olympics is one of the high secure events in the world since the Red Army terrorist attack on the Israeli Olympic team in 1972 in Munich.

Each person entering the village had to be accredited and you had to wear the tag with your photo around your neck when entering through security, which looked like an airport terminal where you and your luggage were screened. We arrived just before the Games started and left as it finished. We had no accreditation and trusted God for access.

The Olympics lasted for 26 days. Every day we went into Barcelona by train to the village.

We entered through security without any passes and worked in the village, mingling with athletes and sharing the Gospel with those who were willing to listen.

We were doing this for about 2 weeks unhindered when the security team at the village changed and we were unceremoniously removed by them from the village. We realized we had unfinished business. God mandated us to minister at the Olympics and we were being hindered by the enemy. We gathered together as a team, just outside the security gate where we were just evicted and prayed. As He has done in the past, we asked God that as He closed the eyes of border guards when Bibles were smuggled into countries where it was forbidden, He do the same for us.

It was amazing to see the faith of those young people rise when we marched past those guards that have just thrown us out of the village. We had the same scrutiny as the persons ahead of us. They were blinded to the fact that we had no accreditation to offer. We marched back into the village. Their eyes stayed shut for the rest of the Games and we could daily come and go and do the work we were called to do.

CAPE BEAST 1,000 – 2019

The Cape Beast is a non-stop 1,000 km, self-sustained cycling event. We were busy with the return leg in 2019 when God did a miracle when I was in need. I asked Him and He granted it just so I could testify about it.

Our route was from Cape Town through the Klein Karoo over Bainskloof, Wildehondskloof, Huisrivier and Robinson passes up to Hartenbos, where we turned around and returned the same way. It was more than 11,000 m of climbing over this distance. The towns on the route were in and far between for provisions like food and water. A massive storm was predicted and with the front rain and snow was expected. We hit the wind of this front between Ladismith and Barrydale.

The safety vehicle returned from Barrydale to inform me and Mark Shuter, who were the leaders of the event at the time, that we might need to turn around because ahead of us was a massive sandstorm that caused safety issues for visibility and breathing. There was no way that I was going to turn around. I was extremely low on water and since Ronnie's Sex shop was closing at 17:00 we needed to rush to get there in time since that was the only place left on the route with the possibility of filling our bottles.

I decided to press on and started speaking to God, telling Him that I trust Him fully to do a miracle to get us through this sandstorm. As He took the Israelites through the Red Sea and Jordan river by opening up the waters for them, I expected Him to do the same for us in this dust storm. My faith was such that I shall enter the storm and expect an invisible wall to keep any dust and sand from coming across the road, allowing us a safe passage.

Ahead of us was a valley that looked like an ancient river bed. For about a kilometre wide there was a thick impenetrable dust cloud blowing down the valley. I said nothing to Mark who was on my wheel about my conversation and intention. I just kept on riding towards the storm. I did not want any contamination of faith if he would not be in agreement. As we

This blinding dust storm in the Klein Karoo opened miraculously like the Red sea during the Audax 1,000.

entered the dust streamer, we had a bubble of pure clean air around and ahead of us and as we continued the storm closed in again directly behind us.

What we could not see from far off was that this storm consisted of two streamers, causing two dust storms down the valley. We passed through the first one and into the open. Ahead of us was the second dust bowl of about 500 m wide. We were now encircled with the dust before us and behind us. I reminded myself of Peter who focused on the waves and not on the instruction to walk on the water. It would now mean eating and breathing dust either way if I entertained any doubt because we were encircled.

We entered the second streamer and the same happened. God gave us a clean and safe passage to the other side. Mark and I stopped, awed by what just happened and took a video of the scene behind us. It just amazes me how God is intensely involved in our little, unimportant things, even our sport, just to show His power and caring for us. More and more I come to the realisation that God wants to be a near God, not a far off God, who is only met in a church. God intervenes in our everyday events. It pleases Him when we trust Him.

3. ANGELIC VISITATIONS

THE SPIRITUAL WORLD is more real than the visible, natural world. This is the environment of celestial beings, which we shall encounter once we transfer from this life to the next. In essence, we are all spirit beings. We are spirits who temporarily stay in human bodies, whilst we are on earth.

In the Bible, we are told that, without us knowing, we could be hosting angels. Angels would thus appear in visible human form and look like humans and interact with us. Angels are ministering spirits. They minister to humans at God's bidding. Throughout the ages, there are records of how God used angels to speak to man and to do something in the lives of people. Many of us might have interacted with angels and did not know it.

I believe a particular sensitivity and perception is needed to grasp when this occurs. I had these visitations, not that I sought them, but God deemed them necessary in His plan with me. The angelic visitations I know of were fleeting, short in time, but lasting in effect.

As real as angels are, so are demonic beings, the fallen angels who have opposed God with Lucifer. They interact with human beings in the same way, but with the purpose to do the bidding of Satan and opposing God and undo the purposes of God on earth. Of this, I have testimonies too.

ANGELIC VISITATION IN AN ACCRA STREET
During a business trip to Ghana in 1996 where I was walking the streets of Accra daily, I came to experience human squalor closely. On this particular day, I was in a throng of people and as I crossed the street, I felt a little hand take my hand and as I looked down it was a little girl of less than 8 or 9 years old who was holding on and walking with me across the street as if it was the most natural thing in the world. She wasn't a beggar as many of the children there were, but someone who had this smiling face and a 'knowing' expression. Under normal circumstances I would have found it a bit embarrassing, walking with someone else's child on hand in a foreign city, going nowhere in particular. It would have been easy to have dismissed her and sent her away.

What caught my spiritual attention was what happened to me whilst she was holding my hand and walking with me. I had a sense of faith rising in me. The Holy Spirit was making me aware of something in a profound way. I heard this message. For faith to be effective, it has to be childlike, just as this child is holding your hand, having no demands or prerequisites, just trusting. The person on my hand had no demand from me, no expectation to receive a handout. She was just accompanying me. When I reached the other side of the street she was still holding on. She had not been looking for an adult for safety to cross a street. By now I felt a bit awkward, a white man walking off with a black girl. I could imagine the stares. I stopped, bent down, asked her name and bid her goodbye.

Normally children play in a neighbourhood and are known to one another. When I later returned to meet her again, possibly craving the same encounter I had before, I could not find her. Nobody knew her and nobody fit the description. This then made me consider what I experienced as an angelic encounter.

If this was the only encounter of this kind that I ever had, I might have had room for doubt whether it was really real and not just a mushy emotional experience. Mushy, emotional experiences pass. This encounter left an indelible impression in my spirit. Whenever I want to refer to how childlike faith feels, this is it. I believe God used an angel in a busy Accra street to teach me something of eventual importance.

ANGELIC VISITATION DURING A WORLD RECORD ATTEMPT

In 1992 I broke the 12 and 24-hour cycling endurance world records on Gerotek, the high-speed vehicle testing track, in Pretoria. I purposefully did not break it with a large margin, because I wanted to break the record again. In 1993 I had another attempt at it. This time I wanted to push it over 1,000 km. What I did not reckon with was encountering three summer highveld thunderstorms during the night, making the track waterlogged and slowing me down tremendously, due to lack of visibility and having to ride wider on the track to avoid the water, accumulating on the inside of the track.

My strategy was to ride at a constant effort for 24 hours. Our test trials indicated a physical effort of 2 mMol lactate as sustainable for this period. That was the equivalent of 320 Watts (NP) and a heart rate of 125 bpm. At that time only speed and heart rate monitors were available. My pit crew supplied me with additional information from the inside of the track.

The first 6 hours were covered at a pace of an average of 50 km/h and the 12-hour mark was reached at around 48 km/h. This effort was spot on with our planning. However, due to the thunderstorms and rain, my speed started dropping significantly. With an hour to go, it had dropped to world record pace of just over 37 km/h when I got a flat in my rear wheel.

The rule states that you cannot receive outside help except in the pit area. The Gerotek High Speed vehicle testing track is 3 km long. I had to run with my bicycle for more than a km to get another wheel. This brought my average pace down to equal world record pace.

By now I was struggling with dehydration and fatigue in general. I was struggling to maintain 37 km/h. To add insult to injury I got a slow puncture 15 min before the 24 hours would be over. The wheel change was not fast as no one in the pits expected me to puncture again. When I got going, I had a couple of minutes left and was behind world record pace and slowing down.

The local Pretoria radio station, Radio Jacaranda, was regularly broadcasting my progress. This drew spectators from Pretoria and Johannesburg to the track. There was suspense and drama because it seemed that the record attempt was going to have a cruel ending.

As I departed, after the wheel change, with 15 minutes to go, I called on God, reminding Him why I was doing this: not for my glory but for a stage to share His power and greatness. 'Now, since the people around the track know I am a Christian, will He not honour Himself by doing something supernatural?' I asked Him.

Gerotek is a 3 km long track that goes through a cutting in the mountain. On the inside of the track, metal barriers are preventing one from riding off the track and should a cyclist do so, it could be disastrous.

It takes the best part of a km to get up to speed. Suddenly I felt a surge in speed that made my head whip backwards and I accelerated to over 50 km/h. I was wary of a wind funnelling through the cutting, pushing me from behind and pushing me into the barriers, but the grass on the inside of the track was not moving. There was no wind. I soft pedalled and once again I accelerated to over 50 km/h. I started wondering what was going on? I checked my dials. My heart rate was normal. It was not me producing an extra effort. I reckoned that if the wind, which I could not see, is blowing me down the back straight it should be against me in the home straight.

When I came in the home straight, I soft pedalled again. Again, I accelerated past 50 km/h without any change in heart rate. Then I knew! God was doing something supernatural!

I broke my world record with 2 km (904.887 km) and continued to set the 1,000 km world record in the same ride. The 24-hr record was improved with the smallest of margins, with about 0.002%. I stopped at the pits and excitedly told the crew and spectators that something supernatural just occurred. They did not seem surprised. They then told me their version of events.

As I departed, they had a vehicle follow me on the track in case I had another mechanical. My friend and team supervisor, Eddie Kriel, climbed into the vehicle. The driver then said to Eddie, 'Well Eddie, now you will have to say a prayer'. Eddie's response was, 'Lord, send an angel to push Wimpie.'

ANGELIC VISITATION DURING A 50 DAY FAST

I am aware, as many other Christians, of the spiritual value of fasting. In 2001, during a 50 day fast, I had an angel minister to me during the night, as Daniel had an angel minister to him during his fast.

During this period in our life, we were experiencing severe financial hardship. I have lost my income and for 18 months we had to rely on the salary of a temporary post of my wife at the University of Stellenbosch. This was not enough to supply even for the basic needs. We already exhausted all possible reserves. However, in the storm, I experienced the peace of God and Him showing me a much bigger picture than what I could imagine. I sensed that the storm was necessary to educate me on spiritual matters and to develop my spiritual senses and giftings, which I otherwise would never get to develop.

He instructed my wife and I to go on a Jubilee fast, which lasted 50 days. This was a personal instruction and not in any way prescriptive for other believers. We only drank liquid. During this period I kept training and even ran the Cape Town marathon in this fasted state. After a while, due to the lack of eating roughage, the texture of my mouth became like cotton balls and looked like thrush. The cells that would normally be scraped off and replaced, were not. Energy and endurance levels decreased over time. I could measure this by the slower times I was running on a 10 km route in my neighbourhood.

On day 30, in the midnight hours, I became aware of a Godly presence in the room. I was lying on my right-hand side. Unexpectedly, I felt fluid running down my back from a spot as big as the surface of the tip of someone's finger. I thought I started bleeding because if I have had sweated it would have been over my whole body. I asked my wife to make sure it wasn't blood. As I lay there, in about 5 minutes, the texture of my mouth changed. I could feel the energy flowing into my body. My body was restored completely. I felt the touch of God and I knew I was being ministered to by an angelic being.

That morning at 0500 when I went out for my run, I was a transformed person. I had limitless energy. For the next 20 days, I ran personal bests on my 10 km route of 10 mins faster than I normally did. The moment I started eating again on day 50, my time dropped to the original 'fast' times, before the fast.

The importance of this angelic encounter confirmed that God is intensely aware of my life and circumstances and would use even angels to minister to me and strengthen me. The picture that comes to mind of this event is the finger of E.T. glowing and Michelangelo's painting of 'The creation of Adam' or 'The finger of God', where God reaches out from heaven to the finger of Adam. I just needed a touch of God. That was enough.

Our financial breakthrough arrived. The instructed Jubilee fast delivered its results. I became much more sensitive to the voice and promptings of God. He removed callouses from my heart so that the prophetic and teaching gifts could be revealed.

ANGELIC VISITATION DURING AN ATTACK ON MY LIFE

I have received several prophecies in my life. I warfare with them. I remind the enemy and myself what God has to say about me. It gives me hope when I cannot see on the other side of the horizon, because a prophecy is like a periscope that helps you see from below the surface of circumstances.

One such prophecy is that I shall become an old man and that I shall be healthy till the end because God has added years to my life. E.g., during my bicycle accident, where I crashed full speed into a car that turned in front of me, this prophecy assured me in that split second before I hit the car that I shall survive the accident. I shall be healthy and not disabled. This 'knowing' made the difference between choosing life over death.

Fighting with my prophecy occurred again a couple of months later, during an incident in Khayelitsha and where angels saved me miraculously from certain death.

SA has always been a dangerous place to live in. This has been so for centuries. Without proper protection, you will not survive. I am not referring to protection by bodyguards or guns, but of spiritual bodyguards and spiritual weapons. On this particular day in August 2014, I went about my normal business tending to business appointments, starting with a local appointment and then ending the day with the collection of some stock for my business, in Muizenberg.

On the way to my second appointment, I got a call about half an hour after leaving, from the receptionist at my first appointment, telling me that I left my briefcase in the parking lot. For some reason, I put my briefcase down at my feet when I unlocked it and climbed into my car. I just drove away with my briefcase looking longingly after me as I disappeared into the sunset. I instructed the receptionist to keep the case with her. I shall collect it later. Inside the briefcase was very valuable content. I normally make the briefcase stand on the front passenger seat with me for easy access.

At the end of the day, I completed my appointments, collected my stock and was on my way back home along the False Bay coastal road, Baden Powell Drive. This road passes the black township of Khayelitsha. The traffic was usual for this time of day, fairly congested, but flowing. At the first turnoff to Khayelitsha, there was a police blockade that directed the traffic into Khayelitsha. There was no indication of why. It could have been due to an accident, road works, public disturbance or any other reason.

Khayelitsha is not a place you do your Sunday afternoon stroll in and thus, even as a cyclist, I am not familiar with the routes. However, the direction the route we were made to turn on to was taking me in the opposite direction of where I was supposed to be going. I took out my phone, switched on my GPS with the instruction to take me home and I started following the phone's instructions.

Suddenly, the Holy Spirit said to me, 'Give your angels instructions now, to protect you'. Having learnt to be obedient to these promptings I immediately did so audibly. By now the roads were void of cars and I was relieved because this helped me to get home quicker. The roads were scattered with cement blocks and in places with branches. I deemed it normal because this is how a slum looks like after all.

As I was passing through a road with shacks on either side, a multitude of people suddenly stormed out at me. I was ambushed. They were an angry mob and started throwing stones and cement blocks at the car. Every time a brick or cement block hit the windscreen, white powdery glass dust exploded into the cabin. I realized that if that gets into my eyes I shall be blinded.

I was looking into the faces of the mob. They had murderous intent. I could not turn around. I was surrounded. They threw rocks right through my 'smash and grab' protected windows. The car doors were forced open and they were looting the car. Several were trying to pull the keys from the ignition and I realised that if they get the keys, I am dead. The rest of the mob was stoning me in the driver's seat of the car with wide-open doors from less than 5 metres away. Any one of the fist-sized rocks would be enough to hit a man unconscious.

During this time, I was as calm as anaesthetics. I knew my angels were commanded to minister on my behalf. I did as the Holy Spirit instructed me 2 minutes ago. I had my prophecy, which I again warfared with. I was going to become an old man and I am going

Stoned by a mob in Khayelitsha and miraculously survived without any injuries.

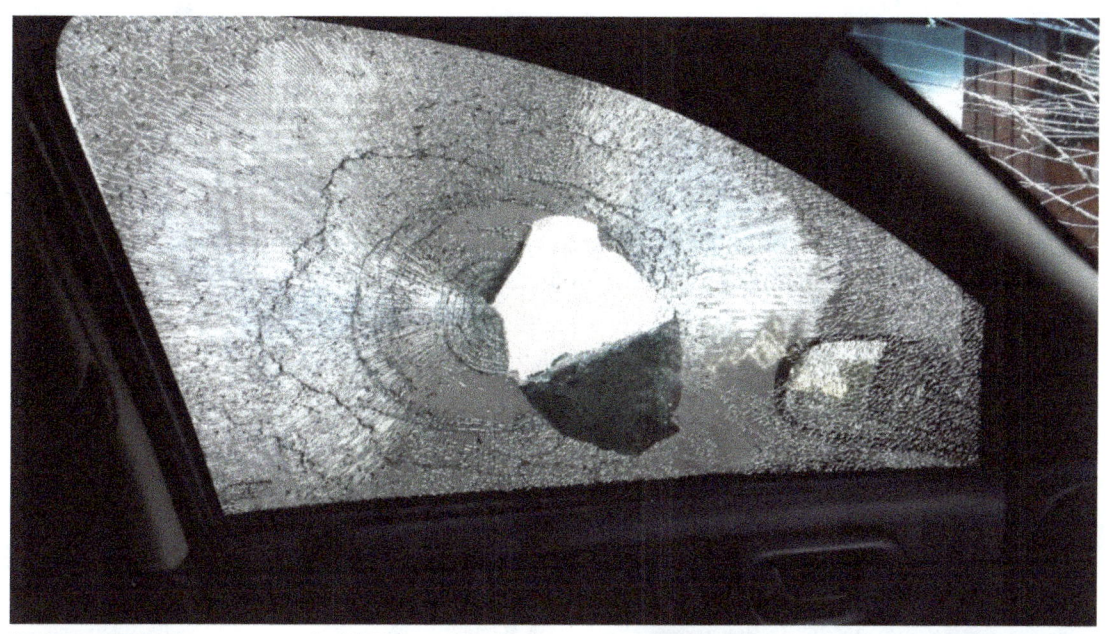

to be healthy in old age. Here is what the angels did. They shielded me so that not one rock hit me. My car, however, looked like it had a severe bout of cellulitis, not a panel or window that was not damaged.

I escaped by getting the car in reverse and with open doors raced backwards for about 500 m before stopping. The last attacker dropped off and underneath the door at around 40 km/h. When I eventually got home, I picked the rocks out of my car and looking at the sizes I realised how close the encounter was and only due to the supernatural intervention of God that I survived.

Coming back to the briefcase. That is of significance. God knew this was going to happen and took care of the details in advance. He took the briefcase with valuable content out of harm's way before it started!

FALLEN ANGEL VISITATION IN BORDEAUX

I was approached by the company, Aerodyne, to attempt to break the existing Hour record of Graeme O'Bree in Bordeaux, France, in 1994. The project took about 5 months of preparation. Parallel to the physical and technical preparation was a spiritual one. I had an intercessory team from different denominations and backgrounds. They had in common to further the Kingdom of God and to do it from any given platform. This record attempt was a platform given and we believed that it should be used to demonstrate the power of God.

In Bordeaux, we stayed in a hotel close to the track. We arrived there just more than a week in advance to familiarise ourselves with the track and to do final preparations. We all knew that this record was the most prestigious in cycling. It was jealously guarded by the UCI. Whoever breaks this record is like the gladiator of ancient Rome. He pays no more taxes and like David, he gets to marry the king's daughter. He becomes a venerated person in the cycling community. With the record comes influence. With influence comes the ability to be a mover and shaker.

Our tests on the track showed that it would be possible to do 53 km for the hour at a sub-maximal heart rate. Whilst we were praying in France the team was praying in SA. My team supervisor and manager was again Eddie Kriel, a dear friend, a former track and road Springbok cyclist, himself pastoring a church in Kuilsriver in Cape Town at the time. He was the first to experience the attack of the enemy. We were trespassing on the enemy's domain and he wanted to let us know that we were not welcome.

The day before the record attempt I was interviewed by French television at the track. They asked several questions about my cycling career and questions of interest for their viewing public. They too asked me about my relationship with God because they heard I was playing Christian music in the stadium. I shared a testimony with them.

That evening, during the news broadcast, the only news of interest was my testimony. We were all watching the news together when suddenly my wife became violently ill and the team wanted to isolate her from me, in case she was contagious. That night, as Eddie was

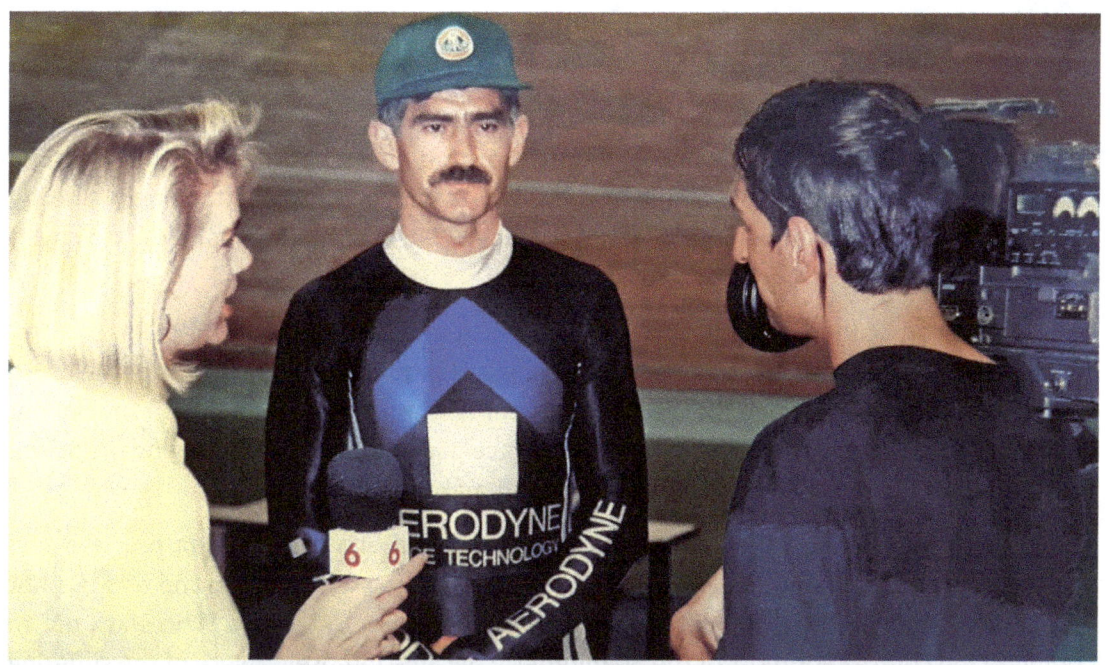

French television broadcasting their interview with Wimpie the evening before the attack on The Hour.

sleeping, an unseen being throttled him, cutting off his air supply. When he called on Jesus, the evil force, which was a demon, fled. We knew the spiritual battle was moving to a climax.

The UCI's change of rule of how a bicycle should look like and which forced us to make unforeseen and forced changes 24 hours before the attempt was another curveball from the enemy. During this time, I kept calm, because it was not my race. A long time ago I already passed it on to God. My undertaking was to give my 100% in preparation and on the day of the record.

For the duration of the Hour, I have never before experienced so much self-inflicted pain. David Butlion, representing Aerodyne, was waving and shouting from the inside of the track. I thought he was encouraging me. I could not hear him as my ears were inside my helmet and my focus was not to drop a heartbeat below race pace. He was in fact flagging me down, trying to make me stop because I was not going to make the target.

The internal conversation that was going on in my head was one seeking reprieve and the other, which reminded me, was that Christ hung on the cross to the end and did not quit halfway through the flogging or whilst carrying His cross to Calvary. Who was I not to complete the course? For most of the 60 minutes, I became intensely aware of the suffering that Christ had during His crucifixion. Due to the changes, we were forced to make on the

saddle I only had 2 cm of contact instead of the previous 7 cm. The lack of spreading the pressure out over a larger area of my butt shut down the lymphatic tubes in my groin. This only reopened due to air pressure change as we came in for landing in Cape Town. Up to that point, I was swelling up like a bullfrog.

During the Hour my prayer team at home prayed for me. In this time the Spirit revealed to them that I was attacked by demons. This was not my revelation. All I experienced was the intense pain, which I deemed worthy of experiencing. Still, when I put the experiences together of Eddie, my wife and the others I realize we were part of a supernatural battle.

Huisgenoot had a field day to ridicule me, claiming my excuse for failure was due to a demonic attack. Luckily, I don't understand French, but I was told their newspapers mocked me too, saying the pastor was crucified on Calvary. I shall wear this too as a badge of honour!

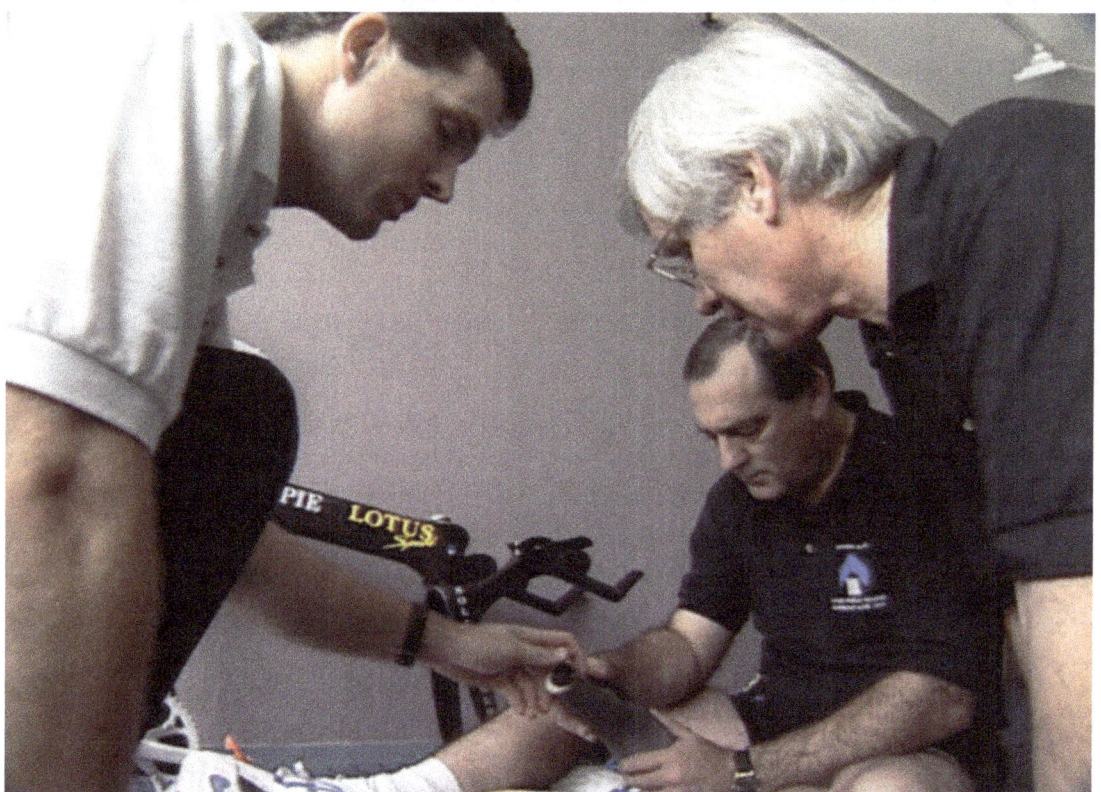

Fltr: Paul de Klerk, Eddie Kriel and David Butlion fulfilling UCI requirements by hacking off the front 5 cm of the bike saddle, compromising the position and eventually the possibility of a world Hour record.

4. THE SCIENTIST

I GREW UP as a child and young man in SA in a time of political turmoil and uncertainty. SA was ostracised as the scum of the world due to its political policies and we were subsequently boycotted on most terrains. The one that affected me most was the sports boycott.

Many times, I have to answer questions like, 'did you ride the Tour de France?' or 'did you compete in the Olympics?' I then have to explain that I could not. I have to live with the big 'What if?' What if I had the opportunity to compete in all these events? What if I could pit myself against the world's best? This just stays a 'What if?'

Due to who I am and how I was brought up I consciously decided not to submit myself to circumstances or somebody else's decrees that attempted to change the way I should live. I do not sulk over 'missed' opportunities. I go out and create them. Early on in my life, I decided to be the author of my life's story because if you are not, someone else will write it for you and you will be living someone else's dream. That would eventually be a life of regret.

When we were eventually readmitted to international sport the selectors of the then SACF made us understand that they would be investing in younger riders from then on, aiming at development for future Olympics. It was a pity. Those teams were not selected on merit but as a future investment. Other countries did not send teams to championships or Olympics, based on the hope that they will be developing depth and experience. They send teams to win medals.

Since I could not select myself for a national team and I was at my prime, I pondered how do I compete against the world's best? The only way for me was to challenge their world records. To me it made sense, no matter when a record was set, you were competing against someone who is the best in that particular event.

Eddy Borysewicz, USA Olympic cycling team coach in the early 80's, taught me that you compete in events that you are good at. I was a good all-rounder that excelled in short and long distances. My psychological preference would lean towards events where the demand for success was due to personal effort and less dependent on luck. A typical sprinter has to depend on a large portion of luck to succeed, the correct lead-out, the right wheel to be on, missing the crashes, etc. Endurance rides, however, is more dependent on your effort and 'honest' riding. That suited me more.

I am not a pure sprinter. Therefore, I was looking for record attempts that lasted at least a couple of minutes. Events from 4,000 m and longer appealed. The real challenges lay in the distances surpassing 12 hours of flat-out effort.

I spoke to Tim Noakes as a renowned physiologist at the University of Cape Town, at the time. I wanted to know what one would use as an energy source for these events? Tim could not supply me with answers and I value his honesty in this regard. The reason for this he said was that there was no research done yet to know for sure what happens after 5 hours when the glycogen stores of the body become depleted. I offered to become a research subject to ride on a stationary bike in his lab for 24 hours if he wanted to do research. He chuckled and said he needed 99 other Wimpie van der Merwes too. Only through the number of test results could they establish trends. There were no 100 Wimpie van der Merwes, unfortunately.

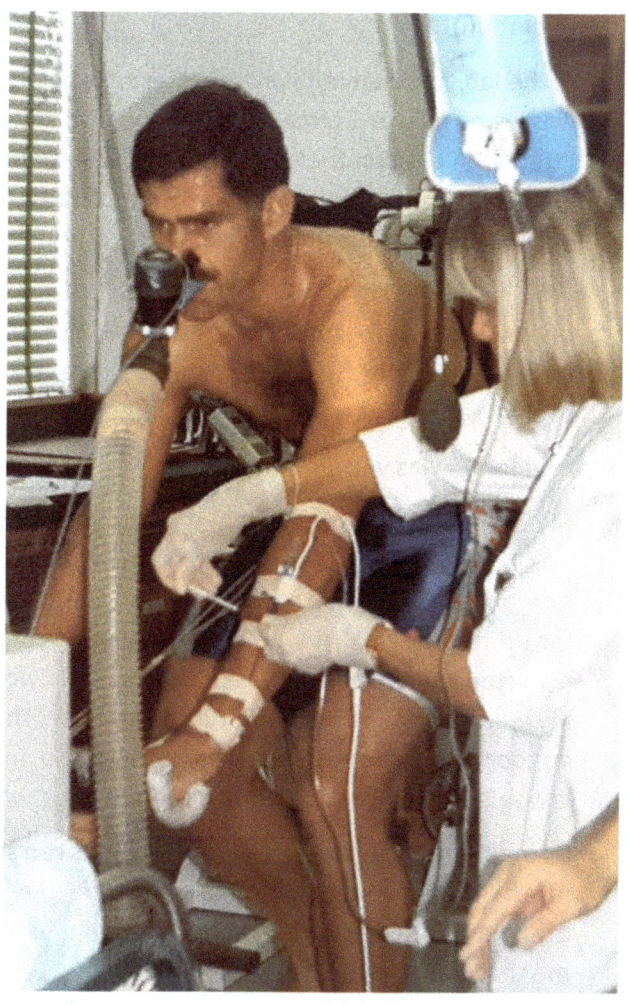

Medical and physiological testing was done at the Stellenbosch Medical School to discover the limits of human performance

He then advised me to become my own scientist and offered an open door to ask my questions and if the lab had an interest in what I was enquiring about, they could help with tests. I was now officially assigned to be a scientist. Today I recommend anyone taking his sport seriously, to become exactly that. Become curious, experiment, ask questions, challenge existing answers and paradigms.

As Noakes commented at a sports symposium, when challenged about the taking of salt tablets and how they could change their stance 180 degrees, he said you should not be afraid to be wrong, as long as you are 'scientifically wrong'. Today I may have changed my viewpoint too on several things, as long as it was justified by results.

We had to overcome certain vital problems and answer several questions in our search for the Holy Grail.

1. Hydration

    In the lab, in a humidity chamber, exercising at 75% of VO2 max effort, we found that I was losing fluid at 5 L/h and could replenish at 3 L/h. This rewrote physiology rules. I was fitted with a rectal thermometer and rode until my core temperature was 0.5 degrees before death. By then I was throwing pizzas on the lab floor. The conclusion was that I was heat resistant due to frequently riding for hours on a stationary bike in my loft, which was not cooled.

    My mixtures were isotonic at about 5%. The carbohydrate and electrolyte content was for hydration, not fuel replacement. Hydrating in the heat was of higher priority than supplying fuel. Dehydration causes a greater performance loss than running empty.

2. Fuel for 'Pay as you Go'

    My caloric expenditure to maintain a consistent 320 W at a 2 mMol lactate heart rate was 1,100 Cal/h. This had to be financed by eating and drinking during the effort at a rate of 1,100 Cal/h as not to run empty. The body can only store energy for activities for up to 5 hours. If I were to take it in the form of liquid it would have to be a very hypertonic mixture, being as thick as syrup! I would have to mix more than 250 g CHO in my water and finish that mixture in an hour. That would be impossible. It would either be too hypertonic or if mixed as isotonic, too much liquid to absorb. At a mixture of 5%, it would mean I need to drink 5 L in the hour which is another impossibility.

    If I took it in the form of solids, which foods can supply this and what would the emptying rate be from the stomach? I have never been a keen eater on the bike, possibly because my nostrils are not flared enough! I should be able to breathe. Chewing does not allow me that.

The option we did not want to consider was to reduce the intensity of the activity to suit the body's ability to finance the activity. We needed a calorie-dense food or a drink that could allow the body to 'pay as you go'.

I put myself a team of knowledgeable people together and in the process became a guinea pig for several years. The Tygerberg Medical School, as a learning institution, had most of the time only sick people to stick needles into. When someone with a Formula 1 body offered himself as a guinea pig, they grabbed the opportunity with both hands. It was a win-win relationship. They were permitted to test what they wanted to as long as I received the results. The Physiology lab under Dr Pieter Fourie became a regular visiting place. With his help, we got some more qualified and interested persons as part of the think tank. We had to solve the problem, as stated.

It was the paediatrician that made the breakthrough. To solve the problem of energy supply for a pay as you go effort, why don't we consider what he does with his baby patients that he tube feeds, he asked? He feeds them MCT oil in the form of grape seed oil. MCT oils have no digestive processes involved. It is absorbed directly and there will be no lactic acid response since there is no CHO involved. The by-products would be heat and water.

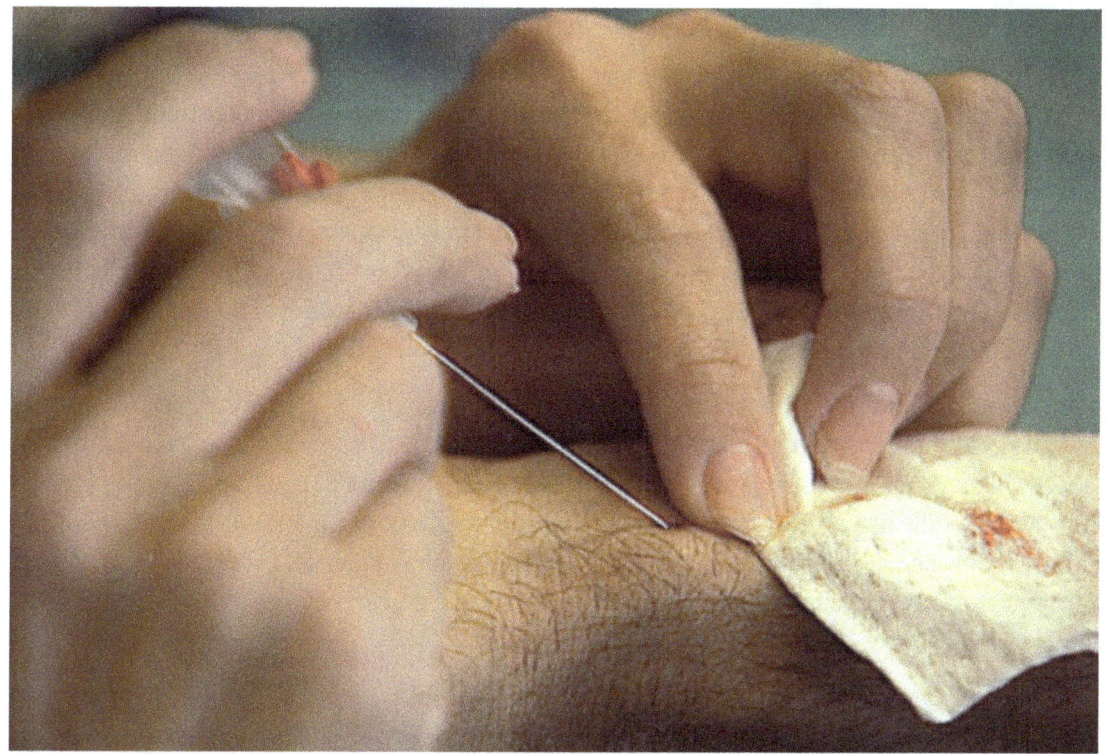

A willing guinea pig has to endure the needles being stuck in him.

The problem was that in 1992 there was no grape seed oil produced in SA. They had to order me a litre from Roussel in France for my upcoming world record attempt on the 12- and 24-hour events. We had no idea how to use it.

Whenever I made a pit stop, I gulped a couple of mouths full down. Later on, it started working like castor oil by softening the stool. There was oil drifting on the water too. This way we knew the rate at which I was taking it was sufficient.

After the two records were broken my body fat measurements were taken. There was no difference. I still had the same body fat percentage. That was an indication that I financed the effort from the MCT oils.

As we progressed in our understanding of the use of oil as a source of fuel, we became aware of parallel sources of information and in this case, it was the bodybuilding fraternity. They were a decade or two ahead of us. They used MCT oils before training to rip. They trained their bodies to use fat as a source of fuel. Whatever you load as energy before physical exercise is what the body is going to use as the source. Give it fuel in the form of CHO and it will use glycogen. Give it fat and it will use body fat. This became the trigger for the concept of Banting. You can lose fat by eating fat. Diabetics can avoid insulin spikes by avoiding CHO, but can use MCT oils as energy to function.

The Americans did experiments in 1984, after the Olympics, on their 'long team'. They had all the vital statistics of each of the 40 riders, power output, blood work, etc. The experiment was to see what happens if they change their diet from the Olympic sports drink diet to one of marbled beef.

For 2 weeks they were fed only marbled beef as fuel. Their performances dropped and blood work changed. After 2 weeks the turning point came. All of them had a power and endurance increase past their previous best. The fat in the marbled beef became their preferred source of energy. The paradigm that fat is a high O2 cost energy source was proven a myth. The secret was and should be understood by those who consider following this route, is that it takes time to adjust the body to a new energy source. Once the body made its adjustments it functions optimally with it.

We solved our problem for the high energy cost of my efforts. Per gram, MCT oils have a higher caloric density than CHO. The additional benefit of consuming fat as a source of energy is that it cannot form lactic acid as an end product. Some of the Tour de France teams now successfully use a ketone supplement as a source of energy. Once we realized that MCT proved itself I started promoting the use of grape seed at talks and soon thereafter wine farmers started producing the oil for the local market. You can now get the oil off the local supermarket shelf.

The use of fat as an energy source did not go down without debate and the ruffling of some feathers. Noakes and his team researched this in 1992 and in 1993 I was asked to speak about this at a symposium in Johannesburg where the dietician of the Transvaal Rugby team would be one of the speakers too. She was on just before me. She told the audience about the benefits of CHO as fuel and how she has gotten the team on Jelly Babies to top up energy. I was just after her and said the opposite. You could hear a pin drop on the carpet.

Tim Noakes was the speaker just after me and he had to be the referee on this issue. He made the following important statement. They receive grants from the Maize Board, Potato Board, etc to produce an energy drink or energy bar from their products. By doing this the maize and potato industry would benefit. Unfortunately, there was no Fat Board.

Companies promoting CHO drinks are not doing our health a favour. It would however be justifiable to have a drink to hydrate the body maximally, but to promote it as the only way to finance the energy for a high heart rate effort is just not true, not in the light of existing evidence and the proof of results delivered with something like MCT oil.

In my attempt on the Hour, my heart rate was recorded during the ride. I was able to delay the onset of fatigue by raising my aerobic-anaerobic threshold, thus my lactate tolerance. During the ride, my average heart rate was 97% of my maximum heart rate. It is proof that you can function at that high intensity without carbohydrates as the main fuel source.

Dieticians at the University of Stellenbosch did a study on my diet and my daily calorie consumption at the height of my endurance training. I always tell people I have worms, justifying why I eat so much. I compete with them. Endurance athletes are possibly the only persons who stand up thinner in the morning than when they went to bed. They did a calculation of my caloric expenditure and found that my basal metabolism was 6,000 Cal/

day and at the height of my training a total of around 14,000 Cal. To be able to feed me this amount of fuel I have to eat calorie-dense food. Someone said I only eat one meal a day: the whole day. Fat is more than double in calorie density and 'takes up less volume' in the stomach too.

A problem that I had difficulty in overcoming was that I was losing body fat. Body fat is valuable as reserve, especially for long events. Since consuming fat trains your body to prefer fat as an energy source, I was constantly depleting my body of fat reserves. I maintained a 4% body fat mass.

As a case study where I can compare the effectiveness of fat vs carbohydrates as sources of energy, I describe the following event in 1994. By then I was quite proficient in my endurance cycling endeavours. I was the 24 hours and 1,000 km world record holder. Someone came up with the idea to challenge a cycling team to race me on my own over the distance from Johannesburg to Cape Town. The Imperial Truck Hire team in Johannesburg accepted my challenge. The date was set for February (in the summer heat). I got a motor home for my backup crew and arranged for a blue light to accompany us as a safety vehicle.

During events like these, I try to expand my knowledge base and use it for experimentation. At that time in sport, carbohydrates were still the 'in thing'. The Potato Board approached me and wanted to know if I would, in conjunction with a medical research team and mobile lab, be willing to use only potatoes during this challenge? The research results would supply

The Imperial Truck Hire team raced Wimpie from Johannesburg to Cape Town in a non-stop race where Wimpie experimented only with potatoes as fuel.

Tripper manufactured the first proto-types of the current hydration packs.

them with information for the development of a drink or energy bar made from potatoes. A couple of weeks before the event I was supplied with freeze-dried potato packs, grated, powdered and in any form I preferred. I was given access to a food technologist that would make my potatoes taste like ice cream if I wanted to! This would be prepared for me in the motor home during the ride.

Today, especially mountain bikers, wear hydration packs. I was possibly the first cyclist in SA to use this by developing concepts with TRIPPER, a manufacturer from Durban, focused on the rowing and water sports market. Initially, I had two one litre bags attached to me, one on my back and one in front of my chest. However, you had to suck and that against gravity, most of the time. The potato sludge did not always cooperate. So, we developed a hydration pack under pressure. You just bite the valve and it squirts down your throat. I carried a 3 Litre pack with me.

Several times it occurred in events that this bag burst, especially when it was still full. You never had an indication if it was over pressurised. The technology was crude and primitive, saline solution bags, used in hospitals were the backbone of it. It was quite a spectacle to see this liquid explosion. Worst of all is that the content was most of the time NOT water, but sticky, sugary mixtures.

To value the full extent of the experiment with potatoes you have to understand the preparation and the hurdles we had to overcome during the challenge.

Something I had to solve was that I could not see through my windscreen during rain or when the sun was directly ahead. I had to circumcise my canopy for vision. This would prevent me from steaming up from the inside at night when the moisture inside the cabin and the cold from outside caused misting. This circumcision was at the expense of aerodynamics but considered essential for safety.

It was the beginning of cell phones and towns were covered partially. KFM radio station was a media sponsor and we wanted to update them as regularly as possible with live updates. Cell phone calls were prohibitively expensive, but we secured a mobile phone sponsor who was willing to part with two phones, one for each team. Going through small Karoo dorpies takes a couple of seconds to pass through. Whoever was to phone from the following motor home had to check when the signal came up on screen and phone KFM, hoping that we would be able to catch them on air, but you pass through so quickly and out of signal range that there was hardly any 'on air' coverage. You just had time to tell the person answering through which town the circus was passing and what the condition the rider was in.

We started at South Gate Mall in Johannesburg and would finish at the newly built mega-Mall, Tygervalley in Bellville. The Imperial Truck Hire team was pumped and ready. The rule was that they could change their rider at any time they wanted. The route was the N1 from Johannesburg and then enter the Boland via Bainskloof.

On this particular day and for the duration of the event we had a very strong North-easterly tailwind, cancelling all my aerodynamic advantages and benefiting the cyclists tremendously. The average speed was 45 km/h for the team. This caused cooling problems for me as no wind was entering the fairing. As part of the research, I had a thermometer in the canopy and was wearing a rectal thermometer for the full duration of the ride. All of this was transmitted to the mobile lab who was drawing blood from me every couple of hours. Temperatures from the tarred road cooked me inside. We were averaging 54 C. No wonder they call this a sauna on wheels!

As we departed, on the first downhill, I left the opponents behind and never saw them again. I was maintaining a good pace to finish the ride to Cape Town in under two days. As the day temperatures were rising and I was dehydrating I realised that I had problems to tend to. By now I knew which mixtures and remedial measures I had to take to address this.

At Hanover we were about 700 km into the ride, I made a pit stop and discussed my condition with the medical team. I was 12 kg below weight and was dehydrated and requested that they put a drip on me. According to them, my blood work indicated no dehydration and a drip was not needed.

My agreement with the sponsors was that I only use potatoes as an energy source. The medical team did not want to confuse the potato data with that of other products like MCT oil. I had potato grits, potato mash, raw potato mix, boiled potatoes, salted potatoes until I felt like a potato. Until today I have built a psychological block to the taste of potatoes. With confidence, I can safely say that potatoes are very effective for weight loss!

I differed with the medical opinion given and decided that under those circumstances, I was endangering my health. To keep the race 'alive' we decided not to let the opponents know that I withdrew but that I was taking a nap.

In the panic that my increasing gap created with the Imperial team, they started riding all together as a team to up the speed and not as individuals anymore. They eventually passed Hanover. Just after Worcester, on their way to Bainskloof, the traffic officer played with their minds, informing them that I was catching up and will pass them soon. This motivated them so much that they increased their average speed further. I believe this is a record that will not be broken easily. They covered the distance between these two cities (1,400 km) in just over a day and a half. The wind helped and the imaginary threat of being overtaken by a non-existent cyclist, who was already waiting for them at Tygervalley!

Once I could not fuel the body on 'pay as you go', I had to rely on body fat as fuel and this was non-existent. You then start using hard-earned muscle tissue as a source of energy. It would have been better to have gained some percentage of body fat, but it seems that it is difficult to do this once your body has been trained to use fat as its preferred source.

BECOMING A HEALTH FUNDI
Early on I made a conscious decision not to use substances harmful to my body to gain an edge on opponents at the expense of my future health. Through my post-graduate studies on the abuse of drugs in sports, the phenomenon of future health problems with abusers was already a known fact. Temporary fame created this way will one day take its revenge by biting you in the butt. One might think you will get away with it, but some of these products have known and unknown long-term effects.

Many of the riders in my peer group I know, who abused substances, are either already dead due to the results of it or have compromised their health so much that they already had to undergo bypasses or have invasive surgery. It is just not worth it. I too, during my quest to improve world records, have undergone drug testing voluntarily. There was no requirement to do so. I just wanted to pre-empt any accusation that might arise in future that I wandered that route and that my records were done with help of illegal substances.

The way to beat my opponents, I decided, was to become fitter than them by being able to ride faster, longer and more frequently than them. To be able to do that I had to recuperate from day to day and from training to training. A good training program balances exercise with the correct amount of rest. If I could recuperate and regenerate in a faster time than opponents, I could repeat or move on to the next training session. I would then have achieved what I set out to do. Is that not the prime motivation for the use of drugs? Because my body does not recuperate fast enough, I need something that can lift me to repeat the needed effort. This is especially true in the Grand Tours where the day-to-day efforts are gruelling and nearly impossible to maintain without some 'external help'.

Another paradigm I addressed was that due to hard training you break down your resistance and your immune system becomes compromised. I have found ways to prove that this does not necessarily have to be true. There are ways to maintain your immunity, especially important when you travel on long haul flights where there could be people on a flight who are ill and you could be infected by them, particularly when travelling to and from events overseas.

The knowledge benefits I gained by working with specialists in their field and always staying inquisitive, challenging the known paradigms, helped me establish a health business. Some cyclists open bike stores, I started a health practice. What was happening with me was something like the development and research that goes into a Formula 1 car. Eventually, the knowledge and benefits are applied to and end up in the local family sedan vehicle. If something works for a super fit sportsman, it should work for the sedentary couch potato. I found that one could be pro-active in one's health not having to become ill and not always having to rely on the reactive part, relying on the medical profession to fix it, once the body is broken.

Health, in the end, is each one's responsibility, not your doctor or medical aid's. We don't have a health problem, but a wisdom problem. I aim to be able, through my health knowledge, to transfer and instil wisdom and understanding of health. When I share my experiences with doctors at meetings, I ask them why they know so little about health and the lifestyle adjustments that could be made to avoid diseases? They answer that they were not taught it. It comes from self-study and attending seminars as I offer.

As part of becoming my scientist I sometimes accidentally stumbled on the uses for products they were not intended for. By experimenting with products, thinking out of the box, I challenged set health paradigms. In the search for natural means to increase stamina, energy levels, immunity, recuperation, etc, you test products and observe. Most of the products out there in the sports arena are promoted by the PR team of a company with a good write-up and linking it to a paid athlete's name. I was never fooled by it because as a sportsman I was part of the scene.

A sportsman's visibility and sport's performances are used as a coat rack to hang and promote products. Many times, the products that worked did not have the budget to sponsor an endorsement. Often, I was using products I had to personally pay for because it was working better than what I was being sponsored with. As they say, 'money talks'. Do not always trust what you see and hear, unless you tried it yourself. Have a critical mindset.

In the area of immunity, I found a product that the US Department of Agriculture tested. They found that a person's immune system can be enhanced by 37% in 21 days by adding at least 3 fruits to your diet with the deep colours of emerald green, red, yellow, orange and blue. The colours in the fruit are super anti-oxidants. These are nature's crayons. They increase white blood cell activity that acts as fighters against the unwelcome intruders that compromise our immunity. Carotenoids and Flavonoids can either be sourced through natural food or supplementation.

We are aware that the nutrient density of food harvested today are not what it should be. Supplementing might be a better safeguard to ensure the constant supply is taken of the correct amount and variety. Tim Noakes has too confirmed with their lab that the oxidative stress going hand in hand with strenuous sport is curbed by these same super anti-oxidants. The benefit is faster recuperation by lessening cellular damage.

Some products that I experimented with had benefits that were never originally intended by the manufacturers, but which I discovered unintentionally. One such product was a product used for toning the body. The target market was overweight ladies. The active components were two amino-acid isolates, arginine and ornithine. These two amino acids, in combination, and in the absence of other amino acids, stimulate the pituitary gland to do what it is supposed to do: form lean tissue and release fat as free fatty acids as fuel for the body.

When using a couple of these tablets I could ride more than 6 hours without taking any fuel on board. It mobilised my fat energy stores. It increased my endurance and saved my glycogen stores. I never become hypo-glycaemic when I use it. This 'fat burning' characteristic is what causes the toning, but the manufacturing company did not know how or why their product worked. The same product affected the creation of creatine in the body. It contained arginine, which is one of the building blocks in red meat and red meat is the richest source of creatine. By increasing the amino-acid isolate intake of arginine one could stimulate the body to form and increase its stores of creatine naturally. Creatine is needed when working in the red zone of high-intensity efforts.

The manufacturers just saw sales soar in SA. They made enquiries as to why the product was selling so well here? Did we have so many fat women? They were then told about my finding and that sportsmen were following my advice. When one of their scientists visited SA we met in Cape Town so he could find out why the product was working. Today it is sold as an endurance enhancing product.

There are a couple of foodstuffs that have successfully been experimented with to delay the onset of fatigue due to various mechanisms in the body, of which one is through lactate buffering.

A South African company, in its effort to overcome potential legal issues with the use and sales of Cannabidiol (CBD), did research to find foodstuff that contains CBD but is not derived from hemp. CBD is famous for its anti-inflammatory and pain-reducing benefits, which is essential for overuse injuries. They found several food sources that contain CBD and subsequently produced a product that could replace the hemp-based product.

I was experiencing other fitness benefits with the use of this alternative, especially at high-intensity efforts. As an example, when you are overtrained, it is not possible to reach your maximum heart rate. You get false heart rate zones and they have to be adjusted downwards to train in the correct zone. However, when I use this product in an overtrained state, my heart rate stays or becomes normal. My training does not have to be adjusted downwards towards recovery. Furthermore, I found that by using the product the body becomes alkalized in a short while. This acts possibly as a lactate buffering agent. Though we do not know exactly how it works yet, we do know that it works. It is for the scientists to follow and see why.

The 2012 British Olympic team's secret weapon was beetroot. Beetroot contains nitrate, which becomes nitric oxide in the mouth once it comes into contact with saliva in your mouth. This is the same substance they give someone who is having a heart attack. It immediately dilates capillaries and increases blood flow to the body and has been proven that it can increase VO2 max by up to 16%. Beetroot benefits the body immediately by reducing lactic acid build-up, helps to convert fat to fuel at a higher rate and dilates capillaries, increasing circulation. Since the nitric oxide is consumed it has to be replenished regularly. The juice of four to five large beetroots will give covering for a couple of hours. Beetroot juice, combined with arginine, is a known energy booster with bodybuilders.

Recuperating and regeneration, not only after exercise but after small or major injuries are crucial for the athlete, especially the one who depends on the income from his sport. My wife was diagnosed with kidney failure and received dialysis. A friend who is a medical sister heard of her condition and introduced her to a natural, plant-based product that stimulates the bone marrow to do what it should do, form stem cells for the body. I took notice of her improvement after just more than a week's use and tried it myself with amazing results.

Stem cells are the master cells of the body. Their function is to replace any kind of cell once it reaches its expiry date, e.g., stomach villi, every 4 days, red blood cells, every 28 days, heart cells, the oldest in the body, every 20 years. The other function is to repair injured tissue. The stem cells react on a chemical SOS, a signal that directs the stem cell directly to where it is needed. The reason we age is that as we lose the ability over time to produce ample stem cells and less regeneration of old tissue takes place. We then start the degenerative process.

The 2010 Nobel prize for medicine was awarded for the research on stem cells. It is old school to transplant organs where the immune system has to be suppressed so no rejection takes place. However, with stem cells, one can grow a new organ on the existing scaffolding in the body. It is even possible to grow you a new organ outside the body that is your own tissue and then plant it in you with no rejection.

Stem cell activity occurs in every person's body for every day of his life. It is not an optional activity, but a necessity. We can enhance it by supplementing to assist what already occurs in the body. By supplementing with stem cell enhancers, I increase my cycling longevity, shorten the duration for the healing of injuries and prevent degenerative conditions from occurring in my body.

During my ultra-endurance adventures, I advise the newbies, who come from a formula 1 road racing scene, arriving with formulations in their drinking bottles and pockets stuffed with gels, asking them, 'what do you do when you run out of all the high-octane fuels?' Since this is a self-sustained event, sometimes lasting non-stop for days, you can only carry

Crude aerodynamic tests with tufts of wool stuck to the side of the fairing.

so much with you, then you run out. You then have to 'feed from the dustbins', by eating normal food you can buy from a take-away or a grocery store you pass. If your body is only accustomed to these exotic mixtures as fuel you are going to have trouble when you are without them. Try to stay as close as possible in finding health and energy solutions to real food and not 'space food'. It is not real food, sucking a meal from a tube. It has its place in emergencies, but should not become the mainstay of your nutrition.

For success on the sports field and to excel therein it is important to heed the advice given to me by Tim Noakes by becoming my own scientist. I would add to it that you have to become a multi-disciplined specialist. You too have to develop the ability to be your own mechanic, coach, engineer, aerodynamicist, sports psychologist, promoter and manager.

5. THE ROADIE

SOME RIDERS BECOME 'King of the Fun rides', but can never podium in the important races. They draw attention to themselves in unimportant events but can never write the big ones behind their name. I, early on in my career, realised that to be the best in a race you have to be rested. That could mean taking a day or two off or doing active rest on the bike, but that comes at a cost. In the process, you become less fit. It is like the snail moving one step ahead and then slipping back two.

Peaking is something you do for big events, events of importance. Anything else is a stepping stone to the big ones. The big ones for me were the title events like the SA championships. You will be remembered as a titleholder, not for winning the weekly, local supermarket event of the town. This might mean winning less prize money in the end, having less newspaper publicity, being less known and having fewer first places on your CV, but by using the lesser events as stepping stones you were prepared the best you could be for the races that counted.

In my career road races were not frequent, mostly every Saturday. If you stayed in the cycling provinces of Southern and Northern Transvaal you could race perhaps on a Saturday in one and the Sunday in the other. The seasons were divided into two, 6 months road racing and 6 months of track racing. This was good in a way. Riders were exposed to both disciplines. If you wanted to ride for 12 months, you had to do both.

At the time of this writing, very few riders in SA have won three senior SA road titles and none four Madison titles. I am fortunate to be one of them. I deemed them important enough to have sacrificed race results in lesser events.

SA ROAD CHAMPIONSHIPS

1982

In the '80s cycling was in an era where everyone was conscious of the weight of their equipment. A bicycle had to be as light as possible. Bicycle and equipment manufacturers promoted the trend. I ended up having plastic Modolo gear levers on my bike since they were the lightest available. The 1982 SA Road champs were held in Port Elizabeth. I represented Western Province. The 180 km race was done on a hilly course that we had to complete several times.

After the first couple of kilometres, my rear derailleur gear lever broke off. I had no spare bike and the race was potentially over for me. It was just a question of time before the hilly stretches came and riders started attacking. Not being able to change gears to meet their attacks would mean eventually falling behind. I requested pliers from my team vehicle to

The collection of national medals.

change gears. Team manager, Eddie Kulsen, found a pair of pliers in his car. The lack of a gear lever to change gears when I needed to left me tactically at a disadvantage, because every time I wanted to shift gears, I had to take the pliers from my cycling jersey's back pocket, change gears and put it back. Had I dropped it, I would not be able to continue.

I had nothing to lose. I had the dream to win my first SA Road title. I did what no one of a sane mind would attempt. I went into a lone break after 80 km, with 100 km left. As I attacked, I was laughed at with sneers of "see you just now!" My opponents, until today, do not know that I had mechanical challenges and that this move was not made out of bravery, but desperation.

Luckily for me, the conditions on the day were very difficult. Port Elizabeth had an uncommon heat wave in winter. Dehydration was the order of the day. I was not the only rider suffering from cramps. I built a substantial lead of a 5-minute gap that I maintained to the end. I did not have the privilege of slipstreaming, nor the support of team vehicles as the peloton did.

Circumstances were not favourable. I changed a challenge into an opportunity for self-discovery. I discovered that I could win races from the front. I had the psychological ability to overcome the cowardice that comes with fatigue and the confidence to discover inner, unfamiliar territories. The discovery I made in this race had a direct impact on my future races and the way I would win them.

WIMPIE VAN DER MERWE of Western Province raises his arms in triumph after winning the South African 180km road race cycling championship today.

V d Merwe wins 180k SA cycle road race

THE senior 180km road cycle race which was the major event in the Mainstay SA Road Championships on the Kragga Kamma circuit today was won by Wimpie van der Merwe of Western Province in 5hrs 4mins 27sec.

Second was Robbie Danielle of Southern Transvaal, who finished five minutes after the winner, with Willie Engelbrecht of Defence close up third.

The cyclists were hampered by the berg wind conditions and half the field of starters failed to finish.

In the junior 100km the two Northern Transvaal riders, Dennis Steyn and Mark Janssen, broke away from the main bunch and rode almost half the distance on their own to finish first and second respectively. Steyn's time was 3hrs 5 mins 47secs.

Third was Craig Palmer of Southern Transvaal, who made a gallant effort to overall the leaders and failed by 42 seconds.

Roy Torres of Southern Transvaal won the juvenile 40km event in 1hr 21mins 48secs. Mark Jantjies of WP was second and Neil Farlie of Southern Transvaal third in a close bunch sprint finish.

1983

In 1982 I won the SA road championship with a broken off plastic gear lever. Do you expect a cyclist to have learnt the lesson that light equipment is not durable? The experience of Port Elizabeth was to repeat itself in the 1983 SA Road championship in Fourways, Johannesburg.

Defending a title is difficult. Opponents do not mind anyone becoming a champion, as long as it is not the same person twice in a row. Having tasted success, the year before and grown in confidence, I waited my turn for the right opportunity to repeat the result.

With 100 of the 180 km left I attacked and escaped with 2 other riders. We built up an uncomfortable small lead. I kept the pace at the threshold and in the process got rid of Springbok Allan Wolhuter and Gavin Mulvenna. The peloton, on the other hand, was not willing to repeat their mistake of the previous year by letting me stay away.

Whilst in my lone break I felt the position of my feet constantly changing and lifting off my pedals. My ultralight aluminium toe-clips, securing my feet to the pedals, broke. My feet were all over the place and not secured to the pedals. I was not able to maintain solid contact with my pedals, needed for rapid acceleration in a sprint. Five km from the finish line I was caught by 7 riders, the top riders in the peloton. It was an unavoidable sprint. I took the brunt of the racing by being in the front for most of the day. They were the fresher ones. They did not know I had broken toe-clips. It would not have made any difference to them, since they wrote me off as wasted and not a contender anymore.

Since I could not make a proper standing acceleration due to my toe-clips not keeping my feet to the pedals, I was compelled to accelerate whilst sitting. I was forced to react to any attack as it occurred, no cat and mouse games. The sprint for the finish was started by Robbie de Villiers with a km to go, by taking a flyer from the back. He was not an exceptionally fast rider, but could maintain a fairly good pace if given a gap and would surely be a danger if left alone. I was onto his wheel like lightning. The attack caught the other 6 by surprise.

The last kilometre contained a downhill and a last 150 m as an uphill finish. Robbie was giving it his all. He then realised that I was on his wheel. As I looked back, I saw that we had a gap of about 15 m and maintaining it. I realised that if Robbie sat up at that point I would have to commit to the sprint and it was still too far away. I decided to use psychology, which worked. I encouraged Robbie from the back, shouting at him that if he kept his effort, he would at least get second place. This kept him thinking and considering. With each moment he was contemplating his options he was bringing us closer to the line for me to start my sprint. As we hit the bottom of the downhill, I had to make my move, because the others were about to enter into my slip and catapulted past me. I could not afford contact. I only had 150 m of an all-out effort and I would have my second SA road title.

Today it is history. I won the sprint with 10 bike lengths. I dug deep into my inner reserves and found reasons why I should succeed. I owed it to myself to reward myself for a season of preparation and sacrifice and a day's effort in front, having worked the hardest of all for this victory. I was not going to submit to circumstances of bad luck and mechanical

Defending my SA road title successfully in Johannesburg in 1983.

disappointments. The suffering of going deep into oxygen debt was going to be rewarded dearly. I shut the voice down in me, begging for reprieve. I made my WHY big enough to overcome the odds.

1986

By 1986 I already had 2 SA road and 4 SA Madison titles on the track, under the belt. I have just come second in the World Road championship in Europe. I was riding for the Defence Force as a province in the SA's that was held over the Cintsa course in East London.

The distance was over 180 km of undulating terrain, not ideally my kind of territory. My preference and tactics with which I wanted to race the opponents were to take the race to them as early as possible, to intimidate and to confuse the opposition.

Dewald Coetzee and I attacked on a downhill and we got about a 30-sec lead. I requested that he do his share, but he felt that with more than 100 km to go, we will not stay ahead. I then attacked him and left him behind. There were no free rides to be given.

I time trialled the final 100 km, realising that the top riders in the peloton had a predicament, the one that I wanted to avoid and that was having to sacrifice myself for someone else, closing the gap on the front rider. They settled to fight it out for the second place. You need not always be the strongest rider to win a race, just the smartest. I finished the race more than 7 minutes ahead of the peloton, my third SA road title.

What we thought would be celebrations soon turned out very sour. Gotty Hansen, the race referee, called me aside and wanted to disqualify me for riding in an aerodynamic skinsuit and not in a Defence Force jersey, which my province did not require of me to wear,

1986 SA Road championship: Gotty Hansen & Arthur Rice attempting to disqualify me for riding in a skinsuit after successfully defending my title. SADF officials present, col Louwtjie Botes and maj Johan van Velden.

incidentally. He was making up rules along the way and Defence Force team management felt he was on a power trip. It cost the highest Defence Force ranking officers present at the championships to get sense into him and Arthur Rice that they were being unfair. My team management had no objections in what clothing I rode and they demanded that any threat of disqualification be lifted.

I learnt never to accept no for an answer. Challenge the status quo. Rules should be there to serve us and not us to serve rules. In the process of challenging the status quo, there will be conflict and disagreements with those who do agree with the status quo. It is impossible to have victory without a battle. The battles are not always on the bike. As a top sportsman, I fought battles against officials, sponsors, sports federations, etc, not only for myself but for those who looked up to me and didn't have the influence and platform I had.

Some of these challenges develop you, some can destroy you. Water eventually reaches the sea. Just continue doing the right things. It will bring forth the needed results. The attitude of officials, who sometimes portray themselves as the untouchables, can become major challenges, which can halt your career. Just catch hold of a bigger dream and reasons to perform than the challenge. This will ignite you and blast you to a different level of commitment. You need perseverance and stubbornness to overcome most challenges, the results of a strong I will and a strong I won't.

1994

By now I was a 36-year-old 'veteran', competing in this category for the first time. Riders over 35 were deemed "veterans". The SA champs were held in Johannesburg. This race was an eye-opener for me on the abuse of power by officials and individuals going on ego trips.

Alan van Heerden was the main contender for the title. A couple of km from the finish Alan launched an attack. I responded by chasing but realised that no one else was willing or able to help close the gap. I just could not shake the peloton off my wheel to initiate a solo effort, going after Van Heerden. I was at risk that I could be expending so much energy that in the end I could not podium and thus decided to rather fight for a sure second place.

I won the sprint, of the group I was in, fairly comfortable, with Anton van der Stadt third overall. As I went over the line, I gave a victory salute with both arms in the air. Gotty Hansen, the race referee, unceremoniously came to me and informed me that I was disqualified because I lifted my hands off the handlebars! I was flabbergasted. It is not as if I am a beginner cyclist, not knowing how to ride a bicycle. I had international racing experience, possibly more than most of the peloton combined and ought to know what is safe and unsafe conduct on a bike. This was a demonstration to me of a man continuously having his knife in for me and applying double standards as Van Heerden went over the line with both arms in the air.

Years later, at the SA Road champs in 2012, in Oudtshoorn, I was in the parking lot close to the race finish, at my car, dressing and putting my bike in the car to leave. The event was already over and hardly any spectators left. It was just officials standing at the finish line.

I put on a branded tracksuit top, ready to leave. Gotty Hansen, one of the officials at the finish, instructed the race referee to fine me with 100 Euros because I was wearing clothing that was not authorised by Cycling SA!

1995

The SA champs were held in Paarl. I competed as a veteran and won gold. This time I kept my hands on the handlebars as the race referee was again Gotty Hansen. The race was held over a course, which took us over the 'Grand Prix' hill, four times, in the Agter Paarl district. I was fairly confident of myself. I had just returned from Europe, having made an unsuccessful bid on the Hour record, in Bordeaux.

In my training for the Hour, I relied heavily on producing my top Wattage and correlating that with heart rate. I only had a heart rate monitor to measure effort. I knew that if I could produce my top Wattage, no other rider would be able to match me, but then this would have to be on the climb. The climb is a km in length and the duration to climb just enough to take all to their limits and into oxygen debt and by stretching the peloton single file, I could snap it and then work with the willing and able. The effort against the climb was thus a sorting process and it would show me who the real contenders for the day were.

By doing this 3 of us got away, myself, Leon Olivier and Anton van der Stadt. I was aware that they knew I was the strongest and I cautioned myself that I should not do most of the work. If the gap becomes too big, any one of them could then just sit wheel and rest themselves for the sprint and myself be surprised from an attack from the back. I saw to it that the gap was large enough, but not safe enough so that each of the other two was compelled to do their share. I wanted the mindset that they would not want to be caught and at least be rewarded with a place on the podium.

As we entered the last km Leon Olivier launched an attack to which I responded immediately. We turned right at a circle onto the wide Boulevard that went over the Berg River. From there it was 400 m to the finish. Leon was at speed and he hoped to use the gap as a buffer between him and the two chasers. The effect of a slipstream is that as you enter it, it catapults and accelerates you faster than the rider in front.

I timed my contact to reach him just as we went into the circle. He was pulling brakes and I was being accelerated past him and possibly because of my criterium experience or prepared to take calculated risks, I kept my speed through the circle and passed him into the final 400 m home stretch. I committed myself to the sprint, so there was no need in looking back. It was all out to the line. Anton, however, sat with a slower rider in front of him as he went through the circle and could only start his pursuit as he passed Leon. By then the gap was too big and all that he could do was to secure his second place.

And did I mention? I kept my hands visibly on the handlebars for Mr Hansen!

2017

I was not racing regularly and only appeared at championship events for 'old time's sake'. Because this event was close to home I decided to licence and participate. Here one meets old competitors and the neo-vets or neo-masters, those people who only took up cycling later in life. It is then when you find out that it is not how old you are that matters, but how many times you were in the ring. You had to watch out for this 'new' generation of cyclists who transitioned from other sports like triathlon or running.

The SA championship was held in Wellington. The temperatures on the day were recorded by myself at 55 C. Many riders suffered heat exhaustion. I competed in the Master's category. Over the years as the groups started progressing towards the older ones we started joking and asked what it would be that they will test us for after a race? Someone suggested it would be for Viagra, heart pacers, false teeth and hearing aids.

In such a Masters race there are normally not many fireworks as it becomes a very tactical race. Different age groups start together, especially male and female mixings. Both try to use the other to their advantage. Our age group's finish boiled down to a sprint finish. Eventual third-place finisher, Linus van Onselen, former age group Mountain Bike world champion, started the sprint. Knowing him from our track years, I expected the move and was onto his wheel immediately. With 100 m to go, I launched my attack, but as I passed him, I hit a cat-eye which caused a front-wheel blowout. I sprinted on the rim to the finish and was pipped on the line for gold. It was a disappointment, but by now I was content just to finish a race and satisfied if I podium.

VARIOUS MEMORIES

My first SA champs were in my home town, Stellenbosch in 1977, which Bobby Nefdt won, Hans Degenaar, fellow Matie student, second and 'old man' Eddie King, third. On the last lap, we were about 9 riders in the leading group. As we were coming through Somerset West, 20 km from the finish, I crashed around a corner, due to a wet, slippery road. I got up, checked myself out for any injuries and as I was to remount there was no bike to be seen. The crew of a service vehicle just threw the bike onto the back of a pick-up and sped off. I was left high and dry to get transport from someone in the following convoy of vehicles!

In 1984 I raced in America for 5 months and just before the SA's raced for a month in Europe, one of the races being the world championship with the Springbok team. I saw to it that I returned to be in time for the championship to defend my road title. I was in very good shape. Due to the packaging of my bike, my saddle post was not tightened securely and during the race, it started slipping.

I was in a breakaway with fellow Springbok Bruce Reynecke. I already knew that with the saddle I would not be able to contend the sprint. With 20 km to go, it was already 5 cm down from the position it should be. I was willing to work and sacrifice gold so I could at least secure silver.

However, due to bad traffic control by the race referee and officials, traffic was allowed to dam up behind the referee's car for the best part of a couple of hundred metres in the

The 1982 Springbok Team. Fltr: Bill Crooney (manager), Robbie de Villiers, Wimpie vd Merwe, Andreas Lehmacher, Jonathan Heard, Martin Lehmacher, Pieter Kemp (manager).

last 3 km. For a cyclist chasing this is heaven on earth, because that means you can get a slip to bridge you across to the breakaway. Instead of that the referee, in the following vehicle, fell back to increase the gap between the vehicles and the escaping group, he maintained his proximity to us as leaders. This allowed the eventual podium finishers to bridge the gap, once they reached the motor convoy. Both Bruce and I were robbed of a gold medal.

One of my 'secret weapons' was training with weights attached around my ankles, 1.5 kg per leg. This was covered under long socks. This was placed under the socks not to hide them, but to prevent them from bouncing up and down my ankles. However, the socks hid them so no one knew I was riding with them. When

My secret weapon, training with 1.5 kg weights on my ankles.

you train with others you acquire a good feel for a cyclist's ability uphill, in a sprint and their level of endurance. This knowledge helps when you have to race against him on weekends.

Nonetheless, I had to take the weights off for races and the results were that I flew away from the same opponents. The word was going around in whispers that I must be on something. I did not rectify the misconception because in their minds they could not beat me since 'I was on something'! This was an expensive way of training because in the process I broke frames and snapped numerous cranks and pedal axles.

1987 VOIE DE LA LIBERTE

I was in the Defence Force in 1987, stationed at Army HQ. The SADF received an invitation from France as a fellow Allied member of WW2, to commemorate the D-Day landings on the Normandy beaches. Ronald Reagan and Margaret Thatcher would be attending the commemorations, as well as other Allied countries' dignitaries. SA was invited to send a contingent of cyclists to participate in the event, Voie de la Liberté, commemorating the 1,200 km route of the battle general Patton fought from Normandy to Bastogne to liberate France from Nazi occupation. This would be done by participating cyclists from the various Allied forces of the time.

The SADF was excited to receive the invitation and immediately accepted through our military attaché in Paris. I was tasked by the Head of the Army to lead this venture. A well-balanced group of about 15 permanent force members and a couple of self-paying national servicemen were selected to participate. We were very excited and everyone started training in earnest. All that we heard was 'riding something similar to the Tour de France'.

We arrived in France and for a couple of days, we oriented ourselves to the place and did some sightseeing of the Normandy coast and visiting Marie St Eglise, reliving the horror of what the greatest generation that lived went through. All 500 riders received the same light blue coloured jerseys. Slowly it became a realization that this was not a race when we saw the "competitors". Most of them possibly participated in the D-Day landings. They were old men, not as young and virile as we were.

We were told that we were riding in columns of about 200 each, with prefects in front, who wore green jerseys. They would keep the correct pace of 27.5 km/h on average for the duration of just more than a week. You may not pass them and had to heed to their instructions. The Garde de Republicaine was to accompany us. The Republican Guard is the motorized police that accompanies dignitaries, like the president, whenever they drive in a motorized cavalcade. They were always on our side. Many of them were women.

The tour was well-timed. By maintaining the pace of exactly 27.5 km/h average the towns, we passed through, knew when to pour the champagne, the major to finish his speech and the cannons to fire in our honour. However, that pace was frustrating. We were expecting a race and came prepared for that. Later on, my team was very frustrated, because they were hardly lifting their heart rate or breaking a sweat. I then instructed them to push the old soldiers who could not keep up. Instead of complaining due to the lack of exercise, rather

Participating in the 1987 Voie de la Liberte event in France with other Allied Forces, commemorating the route general Patton followed from Normandy to the Battle of the Bulge in Bastogne to liberate Europe from Nazi occupation in WWII.

All Provisional medals. *SA Senior road and 4 Madison titles.*

get exercise by pushing these guys, who were falling out at the back. The pace of 27.5 km/h average was quite a feat for them. The South African riders became the sheepdogs of the pack, keeping the sheep together. We had a win-win thing going. At least we got some exercise and the old soldiers were thankful for being pushed on the hills or where they dropped out.

At many of the towns a brief stop would be made, a glass of champagne shared and a couple of words would be said by a dignitary. Obviously, as South Africans, we were shut out of all this because we did not understand French. On this particular stop a long speech was made and one of the lady translators, Sigrid Lecouflé, pressed through the cyclists towards me and said my presence was requested on stage with the top brass. I had no idea what it was all about. I just knew the day before I lowered an upside-down SA flag, readjusted it and hoisted it again, right side up, one that was part of the displayed flags in a town square. I assumed it could be this that got me into trouble.

As I was standing there the speech was made in French and only after the cheers and applause did the translator convey the message. I was to receive on behalf of my team, the gratitude of the whole group, for showing them what camaraderie is, displaying the spirit of cooperation that exists between the Allied Forces. I was honoured because the commendation came from the organisers as well as the Garde de Republicaine. As riders, we had a good laugh about this. We wanted to exercise, but our actions had unintended consequences.

Our unintended camaraderie had ripple effects for months. The SA Embassy in Paris received a letter of commendation from the US contingent, congratulating the embassy with the subtle diplomacy of positive image building through the cycling team. This commendation eventually passed through the head of the Defence Force, gen Geldenhuys, and the Minister of Defence's office, to the team. We were proud to be South Africans and to be Defence Force members. Cycling was not always just about the pride and honour of an individual or team, but a country too.

6. THE TRACKIE

I STARTED FAIRLY late as a cyclist to compete on the track, possibly due to several factors, not having a track bike and never having seen track racing, until the day I arrived at the track to race for the first time.

My cycling started as someone who wanted to enjoy the benefits of cycling, seeing the countryside, riding with friends and doing long, challenging distances. Possibly, since I did not hear that track riding offered this, it did not appeal to me initially.

I was part of the University of Stellenbosch's Matie Cycling Club. Track racing was not a big thing there. In 1978 I was a second-year theological student at Stellenbosch. My home was 1,400 km away in Johannesburg. I decided that for that particular December holiday I shall stay in Stellenbosch.

I got myself a job at Flandria, the local cycle shop, but instead of receiving a salary for the 6 weeks' labour, Danny and Vera Verschaeve, the owners would lodge and feed me. I enjoyed it, because this exposed me to the other side of cycling, the commercial part. This way I could accustom myself to the different cycling components, options available and see how repairs were done.

I could participate in track meetings in the Cape and Paarl, but I did not have a track bike. Through Danny, having contact with other bike shops, he found out that Kriel & Binneman Cycle shop, in Bellville, had a second-hand Cinelli frame. Danny helped me build up the frame and this readied me for track racing.

Decembers were normally a very busy track month. The track itinerary had races on Friday evenings and Saturday afternoons. Sometimes Wednesday evenings were used to accommodate the overflow need for the full Western Province itinerary. I entered for the very prestigious Boxing Day event, held every year on the 26th of December. It was the oldest uninterrupted bicycle event in the world. He who wins that is written up in the annals of cycling history.

For my introduction to the track as a newcomer, I had to be seeded as rider. You start with the 'fish & chips' groups and as you podium, in the lesser event, you are promoted. You could even be promoted in the same meet from C to B, as it happened in my case. I left my first meeting as a B seeded rider.

BOXING DAY 1978

Boxing Day was a day of athletics and cycling, happening simultaneously. The main event for the day, however, was the 25 Mile. There were many filler events, but the crowd came to see the big one at the end.

One of the filler events of the day was the 400 m handicap. The lower seeded riders started in front with a distance handicap of what the race officials deemed you need. Theoretically, it meant that the referee had to determine the handicap so that every rider would arrive at the finish line at the same time.

In the 400 m handicap race you had a thrower. Whilst you are clipped in, your thrower will catapult you into the race and get out of the way as quickly as possible from riders starting behind you. The riders at the back did not mind the handicap, because the rider in front, once he was caught, assured him a slip and thus a catapult past to the front. To benefit from your handicap, which could be 20 m over a 400 m distance, is to assure that you do not get caught to offer a slip, to a rider who started behind you.

I won my first race on the track, the 400 m handicap, with a comfortable margin. This made me eligible to be selected for the last event of the day, the 25 Mile.

I had no clue of any track tactics and how the races were won. All that I could see, from a road cyclist perspective and something I have become a specialist in over years, is to use the wind to my advantage. The Paarl outdoor track was exposed to wind, especially to the reigning South Easter wind, typical of the summertime. It created a gutter effect in the back straight where there was no slipstream. The slipstream would be on the inside of the track, left of the front rider, where no one could benefit from it. This slip started just as you entered the banking after the finish line and ended with 200 m to go. From that point onwards, it creates a slipstream to the following riders on the righthand side, but for the following riders to benefit from it, they had to ride wide and up, to the top of the banking. This caused riders to ride much further than the distance of the event.

As a road cyclist, I intended to make use of this effect. When it is foot to the pedal time, it has to be where no one benefits from your slip and when you follow someone when it is your turn to pace, it has to be when there is a slip for you, behind the rider in front of you.

For the famous 25 Mile, most of the top up-country riders attend the meeting. I did not know them and they, as track purists, did not know me. They might have heard of me, having competed in 2 Rapport Tours by then, but I had no track record.

The race started in front of more than 13,000 people. When the track pavilions and standing place became full, spectators started climbing the trees outside the stadium to watch from there. The atmosphere was electric. It is impossible not to give your best when racing in such a charged atmosphere.

The first half of the race was sorting out, looking at riders who were doing their share, but more importantly, the riders who weren't, because they would be the danger later on.

DIE Paarlse jaer Leon Jonker (links) skiet hier oor die eindstreep vir sy opwindende oorwinning gister in die wedren oor 25 myl by die Gesinsdag-byeenkoms in die Paarl. Stephen Marate (regs) van Welkom was tweede en die Matie Wimpie van der Merwe (middel) derde, Butch Droskie (langs hom) van Wes-Transvaal vierde en Peter Nicholson (agter Jonker) van Yorkshire Wheelers vyfde. Die wentyd was 'n haastige 58 min. 32,4 sek. in die wedren wat deur ses jaers oorheers is ná 'n goeie breekpoging.

Around halfway I decided I have had enough of the cat and mouse games and attacked hard for a couple of laps. This ripped the bunch to pieces and only 4 could stick to my wheel. They were Leon Jonker, Butch Drotskie, Steven Morake and Peter Nicholson, two upcountry riders and two locals from Paarl, besides myself. This is what the crowd wanted. They had local boys to cheer on. Within a couple of laps, we lapped the main bunch and four laps from the finish they were called off as not to interfere.

By then the crowd was on their feet. The people at the fences, with the metal advertising boards attached to it, were thumping it and making a deafening noise. It was an encouragement that could make any mediocre rider perform above his potential. It was pure adrenalin in my veins.

I had already planned my sprint based on my observations of the wind. I shall attack on the bell. With the wind from the right and behind this would give no slip to the rider on my wheel, but I shall only be going at 90%. The moment we hit the 200 m mark where they would start to come over me in the banking, I shall double kick, drawing them down the banking again as I accelerated, into a single file and then into the wind, in the home straight. They had to come over the long way and hopefully, my bike and a half length gap that I am ahead of the second rider would supply me enough distance to stay ahead to the line.

This worked perfectly, until when at 150 m to go, I saw an object, in my side periphery, flying down the banking, right for my wheels. I instinctively backpedalled to avoid anything that could cause me to crash. The object flew past my front wheel and then realized what it was. Someone threw his hat like a Frisbee down the embankment in his excitement. This broke my speed and from out of the back of the 5 men pack I had to reaccelerate.

When Leon Jonker's front wheel hit the line in the first position, with Steven Morake second and myself third, 2 m behind Jonker, I was coming at such a great speed that when Jonker's back wheel went over I passed him into the first position.

This was such a loss. I could have imagined the fairy tale story of someone who just started the track discipline a week before and then winning the biggest cycling event on the South African calendar!

TYPO GRAND PRIX

Three days after the Paarl Boxing Day event the big sprinters' event was held. This gave the up-country riders, who rode on Boxing Day, the possibility to attend this 'Classic'. There were several Grand Prix events over the country and the one Typo Club organised was one of them. Guest riders like Joe (The Bullet) Billet was flown in to compete in this prestigious event. Most sprinters across the country would attend the Grand Prixs due to its importance on the calendar.

On this particular evening, some of the riders who were supposed to ride did not pitch. I was still a B category rider and was asked to fill the numbers. I have never seen a Sprint before, knew no tactics, did not know what gear ratio to select, etc. All I was told was, 'You will be riding two laps. On the last lap, you will get the bell, then you sprint like hell! Time will be taken over the last 200 m and the first man over the line moves on to the next round.' I followed the instructions to the letter.

Initially, the heats were three-ups, strongest matched against weakest and the rides are the best out of three. None of the sprinters worried about me, because I was there to fill the numbers. I won my first heat eliminating the previous year's winner, Jannie Brand and moved on to the quarter-finals. in the quarter-finals, I beat Jannie Nortjé. Some eyebrows lifted and the 'bad form' of my opponents was suggested as the reason.

When I beat the Western Province sprint champion, Herman Kroff, in the semi-finals there was a stir. I won all my heats only one way, from the front and started when the bell rang. Very predictable. By now Joe Billet was already eliminated and I could remember the perplexed expression on his face, a cyclist he has never heard of was beating established sprinters and by further investigation found out that the rider was only cycling on the track for less than a month.

I was instructed by that time not to compete in the filler events anymore as I was in the semi-final of the Grand Prix. Everyone wanted to offer advice for the underdog. It was palpable how the crowd enjoyed the drama unfolding. I ruffled feathers. I was not known as a track rider, had no style or anything to go on except what was seen that night. I was instructed

WIMPIE VAN DER MERWE (regs), nuutste held in Kaapse fietsry, wen sy naelry-uitdun teen Jannie Nortje Vrydagaand in Bellville. Van der Merwe het later gepresteer deur die Grand Prix-titel in te palm.

Paarlse fietsry

WIMPIE GROOT GUNSTELING

Deur ons Fletsryverslaggewer

DIE W.P. se nuwe fietsryheld, Wimpie van der Merwe van die Maties, spring vanmiddag as groot gunsteling

by the chief officials, Hugh Dale to go to one of the spectators, a known trackie, Dougie Penwarden, to get advice. What he told me I could not remember, but I know he suggested I increase my gears with 2 inches to a 90 inch. Graciously he offered me a 50 teeth gear ring so I could get the desired 90 inches.

In the final, I had to race Leon Jonker, who had won the Paarl Boxing Day 25 miles 3 days before. This was going to be an opportunity for payback. Leon was known as a rough rider and did not hesitate to become physical in the ride. He preferred to get on a wheel and kick out of the slip to pass you in the last couple of meters. I was an ideal customer for his style of racing. In track racing you would want to force your opponent to a standstill, if you are in front, to force him to lead you out. There was no need for tactics, I was already doing what he wanted to, giving him a lead out. I beat Leon Jonker in two rides and thus the Grand Prix title.

I was given a huge flower bouquet. What would I do with flowers? I was not married, did not have a girlfriend and was NOT that type of man keeping flowers in a vase in his room at varsity. I passed out all the flowers to the ladies in the stand that night and remember that for weeks later I was still getting winks from ladies, out of the stands, when I passed by!

BOXING DAY 1983

Willie Engelbrecht and I were both riding for the Matie Club. We received a sponsorship to team up for a month and as a team, to participate in the December festive racing in the Cape. We were sponsored by Hugo Lombard. We raced in the blue coloured clothing of Lombardi. Willie and I decided to team up and assure victory in every race we compete in by me supplying the lead-out and him winning the race. We then share the prize money.

We were both selected to ride the 25 Mile. We already secured victory in the filler events we competed in during the day. The modus operandi was that I give Willie as much protection as I could by supplying slipstream and taking him across gaps when they occur. The 25 Mile was Willie's first. He relied on my experience to race it. I especially put a big gear on for the event, about 3 inches more than what I normally raced. I expected a fast race and thus needed the extra inches to match any fast pace.

By now we were known as the 'Blue Train'. Both, announcers at meetings and the press introduced us this way when referring to our teamwork. Since we were very predictable in our way of winning the races: me coming to the front and giving the lead-out for Willie and then him using it to win, other riders were planning strategies to neutralise us. We were aware that this would happen.

W.P.-BYEENKOMS

Wimpie wen naelry

Deur Ons Fietsryverslaggewer

DIE Matie Wimpie van der Merwe het gisteraand in Bellville 'n yslike verrassing gelewer deur Leon Jonker van die Paarl in die eindstryd van Typo se Grand Prix-naelry met 2—1 te klop.

Van der Merwe het 'n groot opskudding veroorsaak deur in die eerste uitdun met verlede jaar se wenner, Jannie Brand van Typo, af te reken. Hy het daarna Jannie Nortjé van Typo in die kwarteindronde geklop voordat hy die W.P. se naelrykampioen, Herman Kroff van die Paarl, in drie ritte in die halfeindronde verslaan het.

Jonker het op sy beurt sy uitdun gewen, maar in die kwarteindronde teen Peter Nicholson van Yorkshire Wheelers verloor. In die halfeindronde het hy weer teen Nicholson te staan gekom en dié keer maklik gewen.

Joe Billett, Springbok van Griekwaland-Wes en een van die gunstelinge vir die Grand Prix, is in sy uitdun deur Nortjé geklop en is in die repechage daarna deur Brand uitgeskakel.

Butch Drotsky van Wes-Transvaal het die Australiese agtervolging oor ses rondtes, wat 'n uitnodigingsnommer was, met 4,1 sek. voor Magemodien Nackerdien van Yorkshire Wheelers gewen.

Chris Willemse van die Paarl was eerste in die 1 500 m vir seniors. Gerrie Theart van Bellville het uit die staanspoor weggebreek, maar Willemse en Darryl Theron van die O.P. het hom dadelik agternagesit en ingehaal. Theron was tweede en Theart derde.

Nackerdien het die puntewedren vir juniors oor tien rondtes met sestien punte teenoor die tien van sy klubmaat Ivan September gewen. Deon Bothma van die Paarl en Niel Buckland van Parow was gelyk derde met ses punte.

DIE Matie-fietsryer Willie Engelbrecht (regs) met die Minnaarbeker wat hy eergisteraand in die 25 myl by die Kersbyeenkoms in die Paarl gewen het. By hom is sy spanmaat Wimpie van der Merwe, wat hom heelpad gehelp het in 'n puik spanpoging. Van der Merwe het tweede oor die eindstreep gejaag.

The 'Blue Train'. Boxing Day 1983 trophy.

Halfway through the 25 Mile race Wiele (Hennie) Wentzel, Allan Wolhuter and Johnny Koen broke away and with this group of willing and able men, established a solid lead of half a lap. Willie started to panic, but I calmed him and instructed him to get on my wheel. Within a lap, I closed the gap on the leaders and the fast procession to the line began. Anyone who wanted to win the race would have to make a surprise attack and create a gap large enough to discourage anyone serious about podium places to chase because closing the gap would cost you a place on the podium. I had no aspirations for the podium because I would be sacrificing myself for the victory of Willie.

With about 4 laps to go one of the local Yorkshire riders launched a surprise attack and gained about a 50 m gap. I realized the typical one lap lead-out was not going to work, it would have to be longer. Three laps before the finish I came to the front and one lap before the bell I put my big gear in motion, strung out the bunch in single file, neutralising any surprise attack, passed the escaping rider and as the bell went for the last lap, I could hear metal against metal as handlebars were banging against one another. The riders behind me were fighting for my wheel. They were trying to fight Willie off my wheel. One of them was fellow Springbok rider, Gary Thomson. To get Willie off my wheel they would have to come past him and try and force themselves in front of him. To come out of the slip at that speed, which was nearly flat out by then, you would be working just as hard as me. I just went faster so they could just drop off like flies.

At the 100m to go mark Willie had not yet passed me and the bunch was still single file. My mind told me that there was a slim possibility that if I double kick and spin that extra rev or two faster, I could win the race! I tried, but Willie beat me with centimetres. It was number one and two for us for the event. Allan Wolhuter was third. Engelbrecht received the Minnaar trophy for the 25 Mile and I the trophy for best rider of the meet.

BOXING DAY 1990

After being 3 years on cycling hiatus my licence was renewed and I could race again. The first track race I entered was the Boxing Day event. I was selected to participate in the 25 Mile. In my absence from the racing scene, nobody knew my current abilities. I had a hunger for competition and somehow this gave me a reason to take the race to my competitors. I knew I had to make the race hard to get rid of the pure sprinters and the wheel sitters. With 36 laps to go five of us escaped, Mark Strydom, Norman Lester, Steven Wolhuter, Barend Uytenbogaardt and myself. Later on, Steve Viljoen caught us and we were six men working together to stay away from a chasing bunch, filled with more professional riders.

We lapped the field and with four laps to go the field had to leave the track so they do not interfere. I stationed myself at the back of the six-man group because I decided to launch a surprise attack from behind from the top of the banking at the 400 m mark.

The attack worked. It caught them completely unaware. At the 300 m mark I was a good 10-15 m ahead of them and at full speed when I suddenly started freewheeling. My first reaction was that I derailed my chain, but that was still secure. I stripped the cog on the thread of the back wheel hub. How disappointed I was as the rest of the group passed me and fought for the podium places. This was a race I should have won. Somehow it was not to be, again. I did not sulk or throw my toys out of the cot.

As I walked across the track to the pavilion to collect my gear and as the public was still celebrating the victory of Mark Strydom, a spectator, an elderly gentleman, came over to me and said something to me that I still value. 'You were supposed to win this race today. However, the way you handled this disappointment carries a greater testimony than had you now been on the top of that podium.'

MADISON PRO SA CHAMPIONSHIP 1982

In 1981 Peter Nicholson and I teamed up for the 50 km SA Madison championship, which was held in Paarl. This was an open event for all. Both Amateurs and Professionals could participate for the title. Our strategy was to take the race to the field. I shall initiate the attacks and establish a lead. Every time I am in the race, I shall increase the lead and when

Peter is in he shall maintain the gap until we lap the field.

Peter became ill the week before the event and was NOT in his usual form. I only found that out as we started the race. He could not maintain any gap I created. Three teams, however (Willemse/Wentzel, Dipple/Barnard, Drotskie/Van Vuuren) made an attack whilst Peter was in the race. They established a lead that I could decrease when I was in, but which Peter lost every time he was in. We were caught between the escaping group and the rest of the field. There was no one able to help close the gap. The team of three must have sensed that we were a threat and they worked together to keep us at bay.

In the process, they lapped the field, went to the front and kept the pace high. They now had the help of the rest of the peloton. This kept us 100-200 m behind in no man's land. The field was eventually called off the track. We were then only 4 teams left. Only honour made me fight back the distance lost by Peter when I went to do my bit. I was not going to be lapped.

WIMPIE VAN DER MERWE, skitterende fietsryer van die Maties, wen hier die Madison by gister se beroepswedren in die Paarl. Chris Willemse, verlede jaar se kampioen, blaas in die Matie se nek. (Foto: Steve Eggington)

I know we were the better pair, so in 1982, I asked Peter to be my Madison partner again. We had a different strategy. As I knew the Paarl track with its windy conditions well, we decided to let me do the sprinting as I was the faster one of us two. I however needed a full lap to sprint and I wanted to be launched at the bell and as the first rider to go into the last lap.

Normally there is plenty of fracases during a mass handover, the potential of crashes and of missing your partner. We had to avoid that at all costs. Peter had to see to it that he was in front and sprinting when he reached the bell. This he did perfectly. I was handed the last lap and was already sprinting when the others were still handing over. I knew the others like

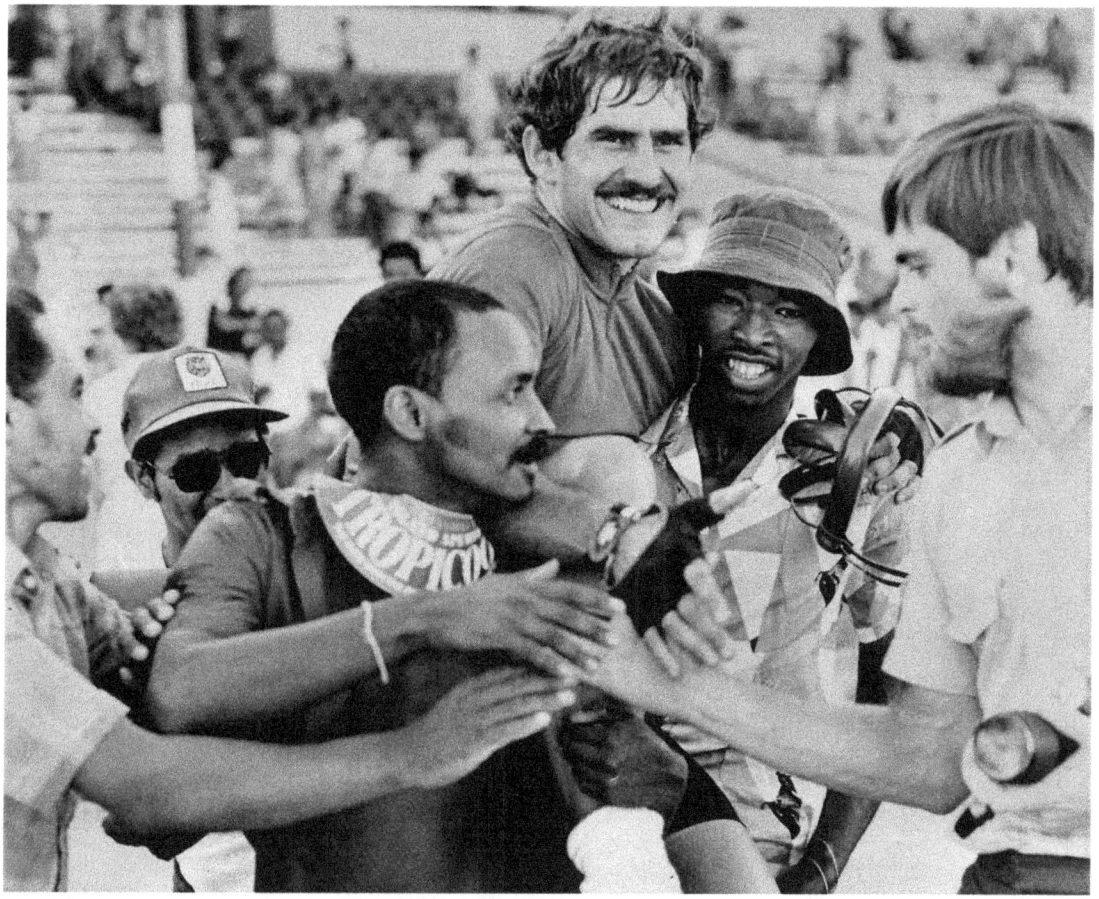

First Pro-Am Madison SA title with Peter Nicholson in 1982.

Chris Willemse, SA champion, who latched on to my wheel, had taken the bait, thinking this was the perfect lead-out handed to him. The wind was South Easterly, blowing down the back straight and from the right, leaving no slipstream for the riders following one another. The top rider on the banking with 150 m to go would have the benefit of coming faster down the embankment and having a slipstream into the home straight.

Out of the corner of my eye, I saw the riders forming the echelon on my right-hand side, up the banking, as we entered the 150 m mark to go. They were just waiting to kick past as we entered the home straight. I had a double kick, a second acceleration planned. That was the trap. As they were about to come past, I accelerated, forcing them down the banking, out of the slip and back into a single file. From there it was the fastest man home. The rest is history. We beat the SA champions on 6 Feb 1982, as we should have the previous year. Revenge is always sweet!

After crossing the line and slowing down in the back straight the crowd poured over the fence onto the track and before I could come to a standstill they grabbed me, bike and all, and carried me shoulder high to the podium. It was an extremely popular win.

[Newspaper clipping from Die Burger, Maandag 7 Februarie, headlined "Peter en Wimpie hou SA titel in WP" — Madison-fietsrybyeenkoms]

PETER NICHOLSON, wat Saterdag in die Paarl saam met sy WP-spanmaat Wimpie van der Merwe die SA madison-fietsrytitel behou het.

MADISON AMATEUR CHAMPIONSHIP 1983

Peter Nicholson and I paired up as a team once again. You tend to study your opponents' style and methods and we knew we were studied too. We assumed that our opponents were making plans to beat us, based on our previous race tactics. We had won a title with me as the sprinter. We revealed that we like to take a full lap as a sprinter's lap.

Peter and I decided that to fool the opposition, we should let him sprint, but only the last 250 m. I shall thus draw the opposition teams' sprinters to mark and match me lap by lap. You just follow what your opponent does. Thus, with two laps to go, I was drawing the sprinters into the race with me. Some more intelligent teams were counting the laps down to the finish and did their calculations, forcing their 'stayer rider' to follow me. That was to my advantage too, because when I started to sprint in the second last lap, going for the bell, two things would happen. I would have dropped the stayer and have a crucial gap into the back straight when I hand over to Peter and if the sprinter had followed me, he would be handing over to the stayer, who is the slower one.

Peter won the sprint and we became South African champions for the second year in a row. As a local rider from Paarl, Peter was celebrated by his community. For me, Peter was a good human being, had good humour and a good work ethic. He was not the typical wheel sucker. When he achieved a podium, you could be assured that he did his share to be there, unlike many sprinters who were opportunists and only won when the dice fell right for a lead-out.

By teaming up with riders like Peter, it endeared me within the coloured community. Whenever I trained through Paarl, they all greeted and cheered for me. I established 'a home crowd' routing for me, especially when the big races like the Rapport Tour entered the Boland area. When you passed through the 'Wine Curtain' into the Boland the cheering changed from 'Ertjies, Ertjies' to 'Wimpie, Wimpie'!

MADISON AMATEUR CHAMPIONSHIP 1984

Willie Engelbrecht became a member of the Matie Cycling club. It made sense to combine two riders from the same club. We had just had a very successful December 1983 where we teamed together and won most of the races, we participated in.

The 1984 amateur championship was held at Pilditch Stadium in Pretoria. Willie and I were one of the favourite teams. There was an upcoming series of tests against an international team and the selectors were looking for who to include in the Springbok team. Everyone

wanted to put their best foot forward. A madison can become a high-risk event, especially when people are inexperienced. It is a speciality event where partners need to know each other well. We were not allowed to hand sling and had to sling either from the saddle or by grabbing the pants when slinging one into the race. Mistakes of lifting the rider and bike up and thus steering him into you or pulling him sideways and not forward are all basic mistakes. I could not afford to crash due to the inexperience of the opposition.

Gary Mandy and I had a big crash during a handover during a madison on the same Pilditch two years before, which left me with a broken scapula and track rash. I kept my injuries a secret as I was to race in a test against a visiting Swiss team and could have been withdrawn from the team had the extent of my injuries been known. It did however affect my performance as I was in pain due to the fracture. Falling again in this championship was not an option.

Halfway through the race Willie and I put the pressure on and built up a half a lap gap. This we maintained right to the end. It was good that we did this because there were numerous crashes in the bunch, one of which involved Gary Mandy again. It was an easy win, not because the opposition was poor, but because we rode the race we decided to.

This was my third SA Madison title in a row.

SA MADISON PRO CHAMPIONSHIP 1984
Willie and I teamed up two weeks after winning the amateur title to race the pro teams in Paarl in front of a home crowd. We were marked as a team. Willie is not known to stay on pre-planned strategies. He reads a race and follows what he feels. I on the other hand need to take initiative and ride the event according to my strengths. A couple of times I attacked

Willie Engelbrecht and myself winning the Pro-Am Madison SA title in Paarl 1984, my 4th Madison SA title.

with the purpose of Willie to at least maintain the lead, but he just went back to the bunch.

We agreed that he would be the sprinter and that handover would be at the bell. When the bell lap came up, I sprinted flat-out so I could give Willie the largest margin possible and a safe journey home. He was the first to start the sprint whilst the others were still handing over. To my shock, he slowed down, let Baron Williams overtake him in the back straight and then latched onto his wheel, but the showman that Willie is, showed the crowd the excellent sprint he had on him, he passed Baron and won with a bike length or two, ahead of Mark Beneke.

This was the second title for Willie and myself and my fourth SA madison title in a row. In 1984 I left for America and Europe to race there and after that went to the Defence Force for my national service and could not secure myself a suitable winning partner again. This was my last SA madison championship.

SPRINGBOK TEAM VS INTERNATIONAL INVITATION TEAM
SA was starved for international track exposure. The Rapport Tour supplied an international presence for the road scene. In 1981 a Swiss team competed in a couple of tests in SA. A Springbok and Federation Team, for which I was selected, was to compete in a triangular meet against the Swiss.

3 Springboks: Springbok track team members Wimpie vd Merwe, Butch Drotskie and Martin Stockigt (RIP).

The Springbok track team of 1984 that did a clean sweep against a visiting international track team.
Fltr: Back: Wimpie van der Merwe, leon Jonker, Butch Drotskie, Manager – Hansen, Martin Stockigt, Gary Mandy. Front: Willie Engelbrecht, Bruce Reynecke, Gary Thompson

In 1984 I was selected to compete on the track for the Springbok team. The team we would compete against would contain several nationalities. As it was the Olympic year, some riders risked their Olympic participation by competing in SA and circumventing the sports boycott. One of these was Freddy Markham. He competed for the USA in the LA Olympics. In that same year, he broke the 4,000 m world record in Gold Rush. I in turn broke his world record in 1991. How little did we know how our paths would cross again.

The other riders were Roberto Silvello (Italy), Stan Tourney (Belgium), Rudi Weeber and Hans Neumeyer (Germany), Gerhard Schönbacher (Austria) and Ben Lyons (Australia). Some of them were established Six-Day racers.

The SA riders for the three tests were me, Leon Jonker, Butch Drotskie, Martin Stockigt, Gary Mandy, Willie Engelbrecht, Bruce Reynecke and Gary Thomson. The team was a well-balanced team, with possibly Martin Stockigt the only specialist on the team.

The three tests were contested in Bellville, Pretoria and Johannesburg. We did a clean sweep.

CYCLING TALES

BELLVILLE MADISON

In the late '70s early '80s, as a newcomer to track racing, we were introduced to Madison racing. My road training partner, Rassie Smit and I were to team up for the madison event on the track for this particular day. We were real roadies. We did not train on the track and the only times we rode our track bikes were when we were at a meeting. An uninformed person needs to understand that when you train for the track you have to do a lot of intervals and sprints. Rassie and I did this on our road bikes on the road.

This is how a sprint or interval session looks like. You accelerate at 100%, keep it there for about 5-10 seconds and then sit up, freewheeling and when you get your breath, you slowly start pedalling again. This you do numerous times. The neuromuscular pathway in the brain is formed: maximal effort, freewheel, catch breath, repeat. With this software programming, we entered our madison.

Somewhere during the race Rassie and I initiated a break, placing us half a lap ahead of the bunch. I was the one to gain the distance on the bunch with my effort and Rassie should keep it, whilst doing his lap. Eventually, we shall lap the bunch. The longer the race became the more exhausted I became and the more I was falling on to my brain's programming of maximal effort, freewheel, catch my breath and repeat. My brain was not wired for the track bike. You cannot freewheel. It throws you like a wild horse if you do.

The Bellville cycling track is built around a dirt athletics track. Next to the track's home straight, on the inside, was the far jump pit. I handed over to Rassie next to this pit. Instinctively I freewheeled to catch my breath. As a result, my horse launched me through the air and I landed like a dud missile into the sandpit. I was okay. This happened in front of the main grandstand, in front of all the spectators and to their enjoyment. Poor old Rassie had to fight to keep the lead whilst a wheel had to be replaced and until I could join the race again. At least we won the race with a slim lead.

WESTERN PROVINCE CHAMPIONSHIP – SPRINT EVENT

As a senior rider, I always had a young rider or two under my wings. This was my way to develop the next generation. As part of my training and mentoring, I exposed them to training, doing alterations and repairs on bikes and repairing my tubulars. In return, for every certain amount repaired they can keep one. This way they kept themselves on the road.

One of these riders was a Stellenbosch schoolboy, Johan Giliomee, from Paul Roos Gimnasium. It was a Western Province championship. I entered several events of which one was the sprint event. As I was passing through the different quarter and semi-finals of different events, I needed to change gearing frequently to suit the event and the opponent I would be riding against. Normally the gearing changed between an 88 and 90-inch gear. I was to ride against Chris Willemse in a heat for the sprint title. I asked Johan to change the gearing for me.

For those who do not understand the rules and tactics of sprinting, here is a brief lesson. The last 200 m of the sprint is timed. The riders have 2 laps in which they can apply tactics to benefit them the most. Some prefer to see their opponent in front of them, others prefer to be in front to control the rider at the back preventing him from making a move of e.g., a long sprint, etc.

Part of the tactics would be to force your opponent to a standstill to make him either come to the front or wait it out in this standing still position. Sometimes a rider falls over and cannot pursue. The race is over for him. Sometimes the standing is for minutes, becoming a test of skill and endurance, especially if the rider in front forced the standstill on the banking.

A further thing is that you are in the ideal position for acceleration when your pedals are horizontal to the ground. If you can get your opponent in the standstill where his pedals are in a vertical position you have that second or two advantage to accelerate away, whilst he is still struggling to overcome the dead spot his cranks were in.

To start the race you have to draw lots. He who wins can choose to lead the first lap or to follow. At the bell, you can start to force your opponent to the front if you wanted to or the rider at the back can pass before the bell rings, if he prefers that position. Willemse won the lot and wanted to be in front because he knew the way I preferred to ride was to ride so fast from the front, with a long sprint, that no one can eventually pass. He wanted to shorten my run-up so that he can pull away and gain a gap that I could not close. Since you sit with a preselected gear your strategy is based on what you can do with that gear. I wanted a big gear for Willemse because I could generate a higher speed than he could, though he had faster acceleration.

When we started on the starter's whistle, I realised something was seriously wrong. Johan put the wrong gears on. I was riding juvenile gears, something like an 81-inch gear. There were no ways in my wildest dreams that I would be able to outsprint Willemse. If he found out that I had this light gear on he would go for the long sprint. I had to force him for a short one.

The experts in the crowd, matching our pedal strokes, as we were progressing at walking pace, realised what was going on. Some were holding their breaths and others were giggling. Normally, when the bell goes, either rider shows his preference whether to ride in front or at the back. Willemse wanted to be in front. The longer he could keep me at a slow pace at the back, the more he would neutralise my long sprint.

With 300 m to go, we were still at a walking pace. He knew he had me. There was no way that I would be able to outsprint him now. His pull-away would be too powerful for me. So, he enjoyed the game. The announcer was giving a running commentary. Eventually, we were approaching the 200 m mark and I went to the front, forcing him to further slow down. He now had the best of two worlds: me in front of him and a short distance to the finish. To him, it was a done deal. We reached the 200 m at walking speed and then I forced him to a standstill in the 200 m, whilst the stopwatches started running. I later heard the announcer say that this will be the slowest ever 200 m on the cycling books.

Suddenly, I accelerated with this juvenile gear away from Chris Willemse and kicked open a gap of nearly 20 m, but he was closing fast once he reached top speed. Fortunately, my gap was sufficient and I beat him with a bike length. We all had a good laugh at Johan's clumsiness. What the crowd loved was the underdog beating the big dog to the bone. I was not known as a sprinter, but still, I beat the sprinter.

7. THE WORLD RECORDS

'I continuously strive to be the best I can be and live an abundant life, a life of contentment, a life of no regrets. I challenge man-made and perceived limits. I challenge the status quo and write my own history.'

HAVING THIS AS a driving and motivational force in my sports career, chasing world records became natural and a way to challenge the status quo. Records were made to be broken. It was an opportunity to challenge the best, write my history and live my dream.

120 HOUR NON-STOP CYCLING WORLD RECORD – 1975

I was a first-year law student, enrolled at RAU and 17 years old when I attempted my first world record. The record attempt was planned on campus, on the parking lot of A-block. The

Willem van der Merwe (centre) of the Rand Afrikaans University, has set a world non-stop cycling record of 120 hours. Willem (19) yesterday broke the old record of 100 hours — set last year by Springbok cyclist Dries Oberholzer — after overcoming swollen ankles and pains in his feet during the last two days of his five-day marathon. The girl who kept him go-

people to oversee the attempt had their base in the middle of the lot, which simultaneously served as pits. The parking lot served advantageous from the perspective that staff and students that came by car would be made aware of Afslaan and the record attempt, creating more publicity in the process.

I cycled for 120 hours and in total, I was awake for about 143 hours. I was completely inexperienced in these matters. When I got up the Friday morning I went to class as normal and only started my attempt at midnight, actually waiting for the time to go by before starting! After I finished, I still had to clear up the pits and take away chairs and furniture before I could cycle back to my bed at the hostel.

The attempt prepared the way for me for future successful endurance events where sleep would be deprived. The event in itself was an experiment, a case study, of which I was not aware. The word spread on campus about me doing this attempt. The psychology department had their informal observers. They wanted to observe the effects of sleep deprivation and when REM (Rapid Eye Movement) sleep sets in. That is when you cannot stay awake anymore and you involuntarily fall asleep. This normally occurs around 75 hours. I was not aware of this phenomenon and ignorance was bliss in this case. I just knew I struggled to stay awake. At one point I fell asleep on the bike and continued riding straight and hit the curb, crashing. I got up, wide awake, but with a dinged front wheel.

The attempt had no luxury of a crew of mechanics or sport scientists or a support crew with a knowledge bank to fall back on to help when entering 'no man's land'. My support crew fed me water when I needed it and the 'koshuis tannies' sent whatever food that could be consumed, whilst riding, from the hostel kitchen. My dinged wheel was taken to 'Mr Bloom' (Harold Bloomfield at Deale & Huth in Northcliff). He dropped the wheel off that evening by bicycle on his way home. That was the extent of the science and technical support.

What got me through the sleep deprivation successfully and which I still apply in my endurance events is to keep the mind 'in gear'. The moment the mind 'clutches out' you fall asleep. The only way to stay awake was to chat. My minders later said I was talking a lot of non-sense and driving them crazy. As the days progressed the circadian cycle flattened. The first few days the need to sleep was intense, but on day three the need was continuous, but not intense. I did not hallucinate, as I would in later ultra-endurance events. Having supporters or minders most of the time, made things easier because you could direct your conversation to them, though most of it was unintelligible gibberish to them.

I later found out that the Guinness World of Records made provision for endurance events of this kind to take 5 mins off for every hour to answer 'nature's call'. I did not know it and thus for five days and nights, I did not relieve myself! That in itself ought to be some record too. For three weeks after the attempt, I was ill due to auto-toxicity. I had to use dynamite sticks as laxatives!

My attempt occurred during the beginning of March, which was late Summer, early Autumn. I was burnt blisters by the sun. Every day the typical High Veld thunderstorm bucketed on me. Somehow that brought some form of cleanliness to my sweat-soaked clothing. The cycling gear I had was primitive to the standards of today. My saddle was an unforgiving plastic saddle, offering no relief for days of sitting on end. I eventually found something that worked. I wound a towel around the saddle and tied it down with string. It was now like riding on a camel's back.

As I was progressing into the fifth day and my minders and overseers saw I was getting close to my limits they called up the newspapers. The journalists of the Star, Beeld and Transvaler visited me to take photos. I was answering their questions as I passed them on the laps. I don't think they could get anything comprehensible from me at that time.

They made me aware that I have already broken Springbok Dries Oberholzer's world record of 111 hours. I intended to ride until I could not anymore. I wanted to explore my limits. I realized that I will never again do this and if that is the case, I had to set a proper mark. When I reached 120 hours it was at midnight, five days later. I wanted to do another 10 hours and then call it quits, but my minders made it very clear that they would take me down by force if needed if I don't stop then.

Not knowing of my future sports career and what would happen in the future, this event taught me various things about life as part of my self-discovery.

After 3 days I was declared medically unfit to continue, due to bad circulation in my legs. I thought I was developing muscles in my ankles and the medical advice was to quit, because "There will be another time". The week before I had my big toes' nails removed on both feet. This was still bandaged in my shoes. I didn't know and nobody told me about wound dressing and the changing thereof. Had I known I might have listened to the experts to quit and I would not have achieved something I could share with my grandchildren one day. There never was 'another time'.

Life is about creating memories, writing your life's story. You shape your future. Do not leave it up to others to create a mediocre and second-hand life for you. Make it authentic and exhilarating. Live and continuously nurture the dream. There is a slumbering giant within each one of us. Potential will not be exposed if it is not ignited.

Success is not determined by circumstances like good or bad luck. You hear of many excuses for people's lack of success. To make excuses for failing is handing over your fate and future to circumstances, to the acts of nature or men.

Let no one piss on your parade. There will be non-achievers who look down on your achievements who are jealous that they did not have the guts to do the same and would rather pull you down and belittle what you do, rather than celebrate with you. Ignore them. Remind them, "Aquila muscas non capit - An eagle does not catch flies".

Years later I realised what happened during this 120-hour record. Some of the world's greatest feats were accomplished by people not smart enough to know they were impossible. Someone once said, "Never tell a person that something cannot be done. God may have been waiting for centuries for somebody ignorant enough of the impossible to do that thing."

GEROTEK 1991

The engineers, Willie Meissner, Mike Kramer and Charl Nieder-Heitmann, in an attempt to improve the speed of a cyclist, built a glider cockpit around a three-wheeler pedal car in 1990. They used a local cyclist, one of my protégés, Hendrik Lemmer, to pedal this over 200 and 500 metres at Wingfield air force base. They were unable to better any records. The Tensor was far too heavy and was made for straight-line racing. It could not corner without rolling. The idea was scrapped to pursue the design further.

In 1991 Willie came to see me and asked if I would be interested in partnering with them as a rider to build a bicycle to win the Argus Cycle Tour? This bicycle would be built based on my size and my input. I agreed. We set the fastest time in the 1992 ACT. This enthused the team and the dream ignited for bigger things. The question was asked whether this bicycle and rider combination could compete among the best in the world? The only way to find out was to attempt to break the world speed records that existed.

On a Sunday afternoon in 1991, on a flat piece of road in Somerset West, we did our unofficial trials over 1 km. Based on what we saw, we were prepared to risk a non-existent reputation. We had an R11,000 mild steel tubing and fibreglass fairing bicycle that weighed about 40 kg, fitted with secondhand, leftover bicycle parts. What we lacked in technical ability, we made up with raw enthusiasm.

We had a small sponsorship from Mobil and Ciba-Geigy. We decided that for us to be able to get any attempt officially recognised it would have to happen under the rules of the International Human Powered Vehicle Association (IHPVA) who presided over such matters.

Freddy Markham (USA) and Gold Rush.

John Stegmann, 'father' of the Argus Cycle Tour and a keen HPV enthusiast was accredited by the IHPVA to act as the official observer in SA for any record attempts. The rules were strict and to have any record approved you had to abide by them.

The only track that could offer us the timing, wind measuring equipment and survey certificates was the High-Speed Vehicle Testing Facility, Gerotek, west of Pretoria. It meant we had to get the bicycle and the whole team there. I drove up with my Peugeot station wagon, with an HPV in the back. The others flew up.

We decided to do a test run on one of the events the 4,000 m flying start the Friday evening, before the big day on November 15. This record was held by Freddy Markham in the 'Gold Rush'. At that time Gold Rush was the benchmark of technology. Du Pont was the sponsor and the bicycle is kept in the Smithsonian Museum for posterity. Our dummy run would enable timekeepers to test their equipment and for the engineers it was an opportunity to see that everything was working on the bike as it should, giving all an opportunity to rectify anything before Saturday's real attempt.

On the first attempt, I broke the world record! None of us expected it to be this definitive. We thought that we were going to make alterations and a lot of tweaking just to get close, but with the ease that we accomplished it meant we could confidently talk with the big boys. One of the crew members phoned the press to inform them that they could be expecting big news the following day and that they should ready themselves to cover it, which they did.

The first world record attempt in 1992. Fltr: Willie Meissner, Wimpie van der Merwe, John Steggman, helper, Mike Kramer

The next morning, as I was leaving my place of residence, on my way to the track, a 'knowing' came over me. I was filled with faith. The verse in Mark 9: 23, where Jesus spoke to the father of the sick child, flowed through my mind, 'all things are possible to him who believes'. I believed.

With our first attempts again, we broke the 4,000 m and 4,000 m flying start. We were elated and decided to try out the menu for other events. We tried out the 200 m and 500 m distances. There were the 200 m with 600 m run-up, 200 m flying start and 500 m flying start. We did not get close to any of those records and only set continental records in all of them. At least we walked away with 2 world records, all set in one day. It was the start of dreaming much bigger.

1992

We held the 4 km world record, but we were uncertain of how fast we were over longer distances. The suspicion was, which later proved true when the plug was tested in a wind tunnel that the design sacrificed aerodynamics for stability in crosswinds. The design was in fact for a bicycle for the Argus Cycle Tour, which was notorious for its wind on the day.

World record at Green Point stadium, Cape Town.

We planned to do the attempt on the 10,000 m world record on the 462.25 m outdoor Green Point cycling track. This track was slow and the sea air thick. At a point it started raining, making the track slippery and dangerous. Despite this, we broke the record. I attempted after that to do a run on the 100 km record, but this was doomed to failure due to technical difficulties with the timekeeping, causing me to restart and me later having a blow-out on the banking after more than an hours' riding and crashing heavily. In the process, I set an African Hour record.

In 1992 SA was readmitted to international sports participation when the sports boycott was lifted. SA could again attend the Olympic Games, the first time since the 1960 Rome Olympics. I had just returned from Barcelona with the SCAS ministry team when I was asked by the engineers whether I would be willing to take over the project?

They accomplished what they wanted to, to win the ACT and to see if they could optimise the human performance on a bicycle by adding aerodynamics. Willie Meissner and Charl Niederheitmann left the project, though Willie was still an enthusiastic supporter. Mike Kramer became the backbone for the technical side of things. Without him, there would have been no HPV and eventually no record attempts. Luckily Mike and I were the same sizes and he could do fitting without me being present.

I became the driver for the project, finding sponsors, dealing with media, deciding the itinerary and deciding the long-term vision for the project. Being an endurance athlete, I wanted to attempt the world records up to 24 hours, which would include the 12-hour mark. We organized the attempt on Gerotek.

The afternoon before the attempt I took the bike out for a spin on the track. I was maintaining a speed of around 60 km/h when my front wheel got railed in the expansion gap between two cement slabs of the track. I could not steer out of the rut and I crashed heavily, sliding quite a distance on my side. The top canopy disengaged from the bottom and I was hanging halfway out the fairing. There was no way I could prevent the abrasions from the track. The bottom half of my left arm had no skin left on the outside. That was the portion that touched the fairing on the inside. As I was the only person on the track I had to tend to my wounds on my own. The next morning, I arrived at the track looking like a half-dressed mummy.

This would be our first long attempt. This was the real deal. This was where sleep deprivation and mind games could be expected. I had the first wearable Polar heart rate monitor that recorded a pulse every minute, but at least gave you a read-out whilst riding. That was my gauge to monitor effort. I had to cycle between 120 and 130 bpm throughout the ride. With a Monark ergometer, we determined that this constituted 320 W. We could expect a drift at that constant heart rate which would end us at ± 280 W after 24 hours. We did not know what speed projections would be, but after 6 hours we were maintaining 50 km/h with ease and no distress, giving us a projected 600 km world record.

However, the use of the MCT oils, functioning as a laxative, forced me to make regular pits stops! This brought the average down and the 12-hour mark gave us a world record distance of 566.974 km.

The 24-hour world record of 815.94 km that I had to break, was fairly low. I surpassed the record with hours to spare. We purposely decided not to break the record too far, because I would be my own opponent from now on. From a marketing point, it was always good to speak with certainty when negotiating sponsorships and when dealing with the media. It kept the project alive in the minds of people when they regularly hear that another world record has been broken. I thus stopped at 902 km. I could have done 1,000 km if I wanted to.

1993

ATTEMPT ON THE HOUR

The Holy Grail of records will always be the One Hour record. At that time the Best Human effort was 75 km/h. We wanted to know how close we could come so we decided to change the design from wing shaped to cigar-shaped. The bike up to this point was a back wheel driven recumbent.

Mike Kramer designed a revolutionary front-wheel-drive bike with small Moulton wheels. The smaller wheels had the disadvantage of not rolling that well but helped to keep the fairing compact and to fit the wheels into a shorter fairing. Still, the design was aimed at having, not the fastest bike, but the most stable bike in crosswinds. The focus was still the Argus Cycle Tour. The bike was not a thoroughbred speedster, but a bike that could be used in all kinds of weather, thus focusing on an all-rounder.

We were always learning and testing thanks to the University of Stellenbosch's Medical School.

Despite the alteration, the team, working closely with the lab, decided we ought to give the Hour record a go at the beginning of April 1993. The lab staff were present at the track and technologist Jabus Wessels fitted me with a breathing mask that covered my nose and mouth completely. This was connected to a pack the size of a car battery, which communicated via telemetry with the equipment Jabus was operating in the following car. This measured my oxygen and CO2 levels during the ride and whether I was operating fully at VO2 max.

The configuration meant that I could not take in any fluid during that period because of the mask over my nose and mouth. This was a great hindrance.

I had 3 Hour efforts that day after breaking the 4,000 m and 10 km world records that were behind my name. Thinking back, that was crazy! One attempt on the Hour is a career-ending effort for those who attempt it. All my efforts that day were red zone efforts. The first Hour attempt was the best (62.9861 km), set in the morning. The second attempt was in the afternoon, after a couple of hours of rest.

During the second attempt, I had a front wheel blow-out and came down heavily. Luckily the carbon fibre Kevlar fairing protected me from serious injuries. I again lost skin on my arm and hip due to falling out of the fairing at over 60 km/h. That evening I attempted a third time but was a km slower than the morning's effort.

Nearly no one outside of the project realises the blood and gore involved in these world record attempts, how many crashes occurred before success. The crew of Apollo 1 died on the launch pad at take-off and it eventually was Apollo 11 that landed a man on the moon. Success does not come with the first effort but after sustained effort. At the time of writing this mark of 62.9861 km is still a SA and continental Best Human effort record.

When looking back at these record attempts, I realise that the successes were largely due to the raw enthusiasm of people who loved thinking out of the box, who wanted to challenge the status quo, and in all of the cases did it for no remuneration, except for the bragging rights that they were part of making history. We were writing history, even if it was only sports history.

24 HOUR AND 1,000 KM

The record was planned for Saturday 20 Nov 1993. We decided to sacrifice the 12-hour record and maintain an average throughout the ride to complete 1,000 km in 24 hours. We had good support from sponsors and media since I had just won 7 gold and 4 silver medals at the International Human Powered Vehicle Speed Championships in Minnesota. I quote from the observer's report for the 24 hours and 1,000 km records that accompanied the record application.

'The observers were Willie Meissner, Tom Thring and Johan van Velden. The attempt started at 09:10 on Saturday morning and finished on Sunday afternoon at 12:53 when the 1,000 km was completed. After the ride, Wimpie underwent a voluntary dope test which was tested by the IOC accredited laboratories of the University of the Orange Free State. The test proved negative for any banned substances. It is felt that this example should be followed by the IHPVA and stated so in the record rules, before acknowledging any records.

For the 24 hour events lighting had to be supplied by a following vehicle.

The race was not without drama. The 24hour record was nearly missed because of three tyre failures in the last hour. Already having to fight back to gain time, lost during the thunderstorms in the afternoon and night, insult was added to injury. With 15 minutes to go the last slow puncture was repaired, leaving an average speed of 47 km/h to equal the record. Racing the last few minutes at 52 km/h, the previous record was eclipsed with less than 2 minutes to go, a too close margin for helpers and spectators who pitched up at the track due to good coverage of the event. The thunderstorms created their own unique after effect, which nearly prevented Van der Merwe from completing the 1,000 km. The mud thrown onto the rider throughout the storms penetrated the cycling shorts and acted as a grinding paste in the groin. The skin was badly chafed and started bleeding towards the end. Only the encouragement of his support crew kept him pressing on.'

The record was improved with 2 km to 904.887 km and the 1,000 km was set at 27:43:48 hrs.

1994

THE FIRST WORLD RECORDS OF THE NEW SA

South Africa was going through political turmoil. For a few years, the country has been going through rolling mass actions where daily murders of black on black occurred and political parties were creating a bleak and uncertain future for the country. This eventually caused millions of mainly white South Africans to flee the country. These would be the people who did not foresee a future in this country anymore, causing a serious brain drain that would eventually lead SA towards a failed state. Mike Kramer was one of the persons who started packing up to leave the country for New Zeeland as the first democratic election was to be held in SA on 27 April 1994.

The last world record attempt in 1994. Fltr: Justus vd Merwe, Dan Oosthuizen, Wimpie vd Merwe, Eddie Kriel, Willem vd Merwe, Gerotek official.

Rupert International had just purchased all my bicycles for their museum. Subsequently, I was without a bicycle for the next world record attempt. In between packing and wrapping up his affairs in SA, Mike had to build a frame for our original first design bicycle, the back wheel driven one. It was a rushed job since nothing was tested before we reached the track at Gerotek. Many alterations needed to be made, which should have been taken care of before the ride, but our date was set and our engineer could unfortunately not work any faster. Our seat and gearing were giving us endless problems. With a couple of my pastor friends who accompanied me to the event from Cape Town, we sorted it out, each doing what his hand could find to do.

As expected, I have become my own worst opponent. I had to break my world records. We were at the track for a couple of days. Conditions had to be ideal for a record to be recognised officially. The wind always had to be under the required speed. During an attempt, when the wind speed rises above the required maximum limit, I had to be flagged down and start over again! I had already expended much energy in the testing of the bike. The first record to fall was the 4,000 m, after several maximal efforts, bringing the mark to 3:33 min. As a matter of interest, this is the record that took the longest to break by my opponents. There was an effort by competitors, due to being unable to break it, to instate records at altitude and records at sea level.

The 10 km, however, gave us headaches. We were missing it with seconds every time and I was becoming drained. I decided to give it a last go in the late afternoon and squeezed an effort out of myself to shave off just a second or two from my record. It was now at 8:39 min, nearly a minute better than my first record for the 10 km, which I set 2 years before on Green Point stadium. As a trivia fact, these two records today are the first world records set in the new South Africa. That was 2 days after the elections and a week before my 37th birthday. That was my last record in the human-powered vehicle.

I was content that I achieved what I wanted to at the time and that I had a team of sponsors and close friends, courageous and enthusiastic enough to believe in the picture I painted before them and to become part of my WHY.

LIST OF WORLD RECORDS
13 Cycling World records - Best Human Performance (BHP)

Event	Record	Year
* 4,000 m flying start	x 1 - 3 min 22.388 sec	(91)
* 4,000 m	x 4 - 3 min 33 sec	(91, 92, 93, 94)
* 10,000 m	x 3 - 8 min 39 sec	(92, 93, 94)
* 12 hours	x 1 - 566.974 km	(92)
* 24 hours	x 2 - 904.887 km	(92, 93)
* 1,000 km	x 1 - 27 hr 43 min 48 sec	(93)
* Non-stop cycling	x 1 - 120 hours	(75)

THE ATTEMPT ON THE UCI HOUR RECORD
In the time from 1992–1994, the Hour record changed ownership between Chris Boardman and Graeme O'Bree like someone trying to hold on to a hot potato.

Chris Boardman made the Lotus bike famous by winning the individual pursuit in world record time at the Barcelona Olympic Games. I had the privilege to view the event from the side of the track. The bicycle was a monocoque structure. Lotus awarded the manufacturing rights to Aerodyne Space Technology, a local South African composites company. As part of their marketing campaign, Lotus wanted someone to set the hour world record on their bike. Through Aerodyne they approached me.

The indoor wooden track in Bordeaux is one of the fastest tracks in the world.

Initially, I declined because I knew this event is for a speedster. I offered them names in the South African cycling fraternity who they could approach, people like Willie Engelbrecht and company. They were adamant to have me. I needed to know why me then? David Butlion, the representative for Aerodyne, replied that he needed someone with the right mental capacity to attempt it since the effort is famous for its level of difficulty. He needed someone with a strong mindset and a proven world record background. At that time, I held the Best Human Performance record for the Hour at over 62.9 km.

With a magnificent backup team from Aerodyne and Lotus, consisting of people with the best skill-sets we calculated that with my aerodynamic drag I needed to give an output of 420 W for the hour. This number was determined after spending 3 days in the CSIR wind tunnel in Pretoria, finding the most aerodynamic position and then building the bike under me into the desired position.

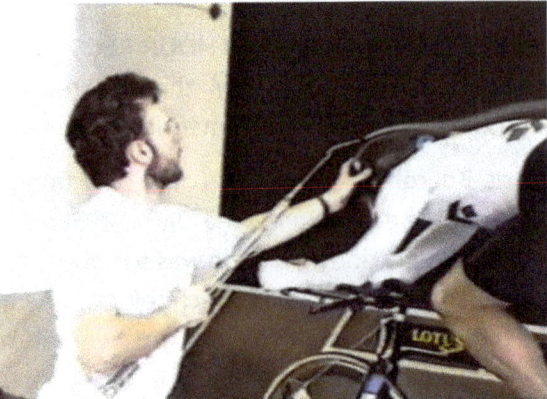

The Lotus aerodynamicist, Richard Hill, was sent over from Britain especially to assist with this task. He worked closely with Chris Boardman during his world record attempt and in preparation for the Barcelona Olympics. They calculated the friction of each moving part of the bicycle, the rolling resistance of tyres and at different tyre pressures, my drag in different air temperatures and surfaces. However, I did not allow them to consider shaving my trademark moustache!

The frame was monocoque in structure. The handlebars originated on the fork crown. The seat position was unchangeable. Only a person with my dimensions would be able to ride it. It was not possible to make any alterations. It was a radical bike, made just for me.

I dedicated 5 months preparing for the event. SA did not have an indoor track and the height of the preparation period was during our rainy wintertime. Much was thus done on simulators, static Watt bikes. Eventually, I could maintain 65 minutes at 425 W at a steady heart rate at around 4 mMol lactate.

We arrived in France 2 weeks before the attempt. My attempt would take place as the first event of a scheduled track meeting. I had the track for 2 weeks to do final preparations. Our daily testing indicated that I would be able to do just over 53 km at a steady heart rate, as predicted. O'Bree's record was 52.713 km, set on 27 April 1994. We were confident of success.

However, a curveball was delivered by the governing UCI who inspected the bike 48 hours before the attempt. The design was illegal. Unknown to us and the sponsors the rules on how a bike should look like were recently changed. The 'washing machine bike' design of O'Bree obliged them to change the rules. My bicycle was a monocoque structure and the

Wimpie and Graeme O'bree spending time together at the 1994 Argus Tour.

Graham Hill looking on as the UCI officials inspect the Lotus bike.

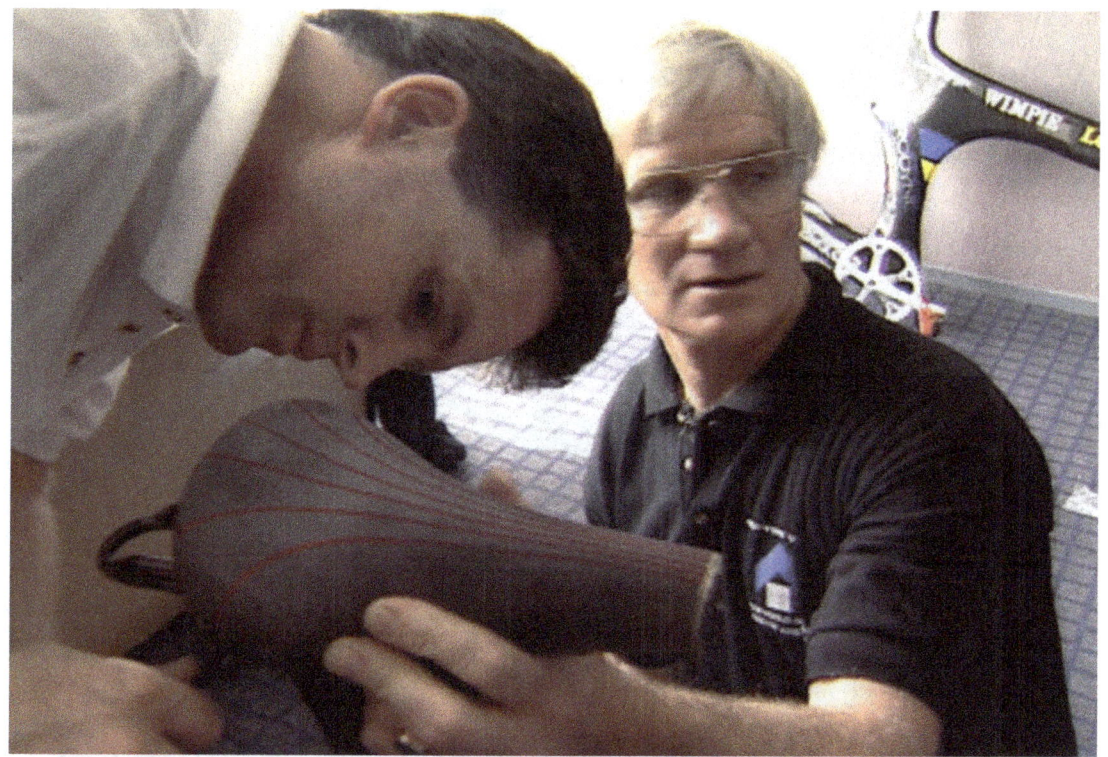
Paul de Klerk and Eddie Kriel 'circumcising' my saddle to fulfil the UCI demand.

saddle position was an integral part of the design and construction. It could not be moved and they wanted the saddle 5 cm backwards, which obviously could not, in my case.

We sat with a huge problem. We got the stadium for free on the condition that the record attempt forms part of a scheduled cycling event on the French cycling calendar. To be able to be part of a legal attempt the bicycle had to be legal because the UCI would not officiate an illegal attempt. Should we decide to go ahead and do the attempt with an illegal design and succeed, there would be the struggle to get the effort recognised later and knowing the UCI, that would be like farting against thunder. Secondly, the unexpected cost implication of staying longer and renting the stadium for an 'illegal' event with non-sanctioned officials, created a near impossibility.

It was 24 hours before the event and the sponsors needed to make difficult decisions. Either way, it would have an impact on the record attempt. They decided to cut 5 cm off the front of the saddle and hopefully it would not impact me much. How wrong they were!

By cutting the nose of the saddle off we found I only had 2 cm contact with the saddle between my legs and no contact with my pelvic bones at the back, making the position unrideable and very painful. The rest is now history. I did not make the desired distance. However, it was good enough for 3 SA records.

Because of not succeeding I suspect the then South African Cycling Federation failed to put the Hour on the books as a SA Record. I broke the long-standing Elite 4,000 m SA record of

Fltr: Eddie Kriel, Richard Hill, Wimpie vd Merwe, David Butlion, Paul de Klerk, Lize de Klerk, Christa vd Merwe.

Andy Theron with the first 4,000 m too, clocking 4:50 during the same ride. At the same time, it was a veteran SA record.

One of my regrets in life lies around this particular and very prestigious record. Hindsight is a perfect science, as they say. Had we done as planned and broken the record of O'Bree and waited a couple of years it might have been recognised as one of the successful attempts on the record's timeline. The rulings on the designs were later relaxed, accommodating the 'Superman position' and the position of O'Bree as part of the UCI's Best Human Performances. This was an opportunity to have had a South African claiming this record, even if it was only for a short period. Miguel Indurain was the next to improve the record on 2 Sept 1994 to 53.04 km.

It was a pity that Aerodyne destroyed the bike after the attempt. I am not sure of the rationale. Today the Lotus club in the UK would give anything to make it part of their collection of unique Lotus bikes.

After my various record attempts and winning several world titles my bicycles were deemed of public interest and historic value and are currently displayed at the Vehicle Museum at L'Ormarins, close to Franschhoek and at the Trail's End Bike museum in Grabouw.

At the IHPV Speed Championships, I was approached by a buyer to acquire my bike. That would solve my problem of packaging and transporting the bike back to SA.

As I arrived back in the country, I got a call from the big boss at Rupert International. He wanted to come and see me. At the meeting he made me understand that I am a very irresponsible person. He asked me how many world record holders and world champions in one person do I think SA had? Only me. Then I go and sell Africana to Americans... He offered to buy all the bicycles I had for the museum on the spot and wanted to know how much I would charge to rebuild the same bicycle I sold in America? He wanted a commitment that when I break my next world record, I would release the bike and they will have it collected from me.

Eventually, they got all the historic bikes, which is now on display in the different museums. When viewing the bikes people observe that everything is low tech, expecting rocket science inside. People do not realize that they were all built on a shoestring budget by non-paid enthusiasts, using self-made and left-over bike parts.

When the plug was analysed for its aerodynamics, in the wind tunnel at the engineering dept of RAU (now University of Johannesburg), they found it to be as aerodynamic as a brick – possibly the same story as that of the Dakota that was also not supposed to fly.

HPV display at L'Ormarins Motor Vehicle museum, Franschhoek.

8. WORLD CHAMPIONSHIPS

SOUTH AFRICA WAS deprived of international participation due to the sports boycott from 1960 – 1992. Though sportsmen hardly had anything to do with politics we were on the receiving side. The boycotting world could not truly say they had a world championship if all were not represented. It is just as ridiculous when the Americans, when pitting local baseball teams against one another call it a world championship or e.g., calling the winning time of a race between two cities a world record!

As South Africans, we had to play with the cards that we were dealt. Where we could circumvent the boycott, we did. From the early '80s, the SA Cycling Federation sent Springbok teams to compete overseas to participate in races of willing federations who were not aligned with the UCI. The 'official' body was compelled by the IOC to enforce the sports boycott against SA. These willing cycling bodies, like the WAOD's, itineraries were used to expose our cyclists to international racing. This built depth and experience within the cycling fraternity and all the fellow cyclists in SA eventually benefitted from it.

Cyclists from my era like Alan van Heerden, Ertjies Bezuidenhout, Robbie McIntosh, Hans Degenaar, etc all participated in events in Europe where they were welcomed by organisers and cycling bodies who did not care for boycotts and politics.

At that time cycling was divided between professional and amateur cyclists. Once you turn professional you could not become an amateur again. This left many pro riders who could not get contracts as professional riders and did not want to race as independent riders high and dry. Many of them did not want to end their cycling careers so they had to find cycling federations that were not aligned with the UCI to be able to continue cycling. At the same time, these bodies welcomed the numbers of the UCI spilling over to them, making their events interesting with known names and increasing their cycling numbers and depth.

It however had a dark side too. The UCI was doing drug testing and when someone was found positive and banned for a couple of years, the riders found themselves welcomed in these alternative bodies where no questions were asked. It did not, however, end the bad habits of the cyclists they were giving a haven to. By no means were the alternative cycling bodies, whom the South Africans were competing against of a lower standard. Many of our opponents were ex-pros and riders who failed drug tests and were possibly still using them.

My determination to compete at the highest level offered to me the opportunity to be the best I could be, to excel, to write my own history, to challenge the 'NO' placed on South Africa to compete internationally and in the process being imposed on me without my permission. When a string is offered to me to pull myself out of a situation I was not going to wait until it one day becomes a rope, but will weave the string till it becomes a rope. I was not going to wait for the world to change, but change the circumstances, imposed on me by the world to pull myself out.

WORLD AMATEUR CYCLING CHAMPIONSHIPS IN EUROPE

1984

In 1984 I did researh for my Master degree in America and raced mainly in Colorado at heights above 7,000 ft. I was in close contact with the American Olympic cycling coaching squad of Eddy Borysewicz at the Olympic Training Centre in Colorado Springs. Interestingly they were prepared to share technical 'secrets' with me before the LA Olympic Games because I was from a country that was a non-participant. I was possibly the first non-American to see the 'Funny bike', the start of the era of mass-produced aerodynamic bikes. They used the small front wheel and large back wheel concept successfully for the team pursuit on the track. It placed the second rider closer to the rider in front of him and thus giving him a larger slipstream and a resultant faster speed. In the 5 months that my wife and I were there, I gained valuable experience.

The racing was immensely hard and mainly criterium races. Olympic teams were sending their riders to Colorado to gain experience and flex their muscles amongst potential Olympic contenders.

My racing was against the calibre riders of Alexi Grewal (Olympic gold), Davis Phinney, Andy Hampsten and I should not omit riders like Connie Carpenter (Olympic gold) and Rebecca Twigg (Olympic silver), female cyclists whose mere presence in the peloton prevented me from quitting. They made things look so easy when my male ego was suffering and contemplating dropping out of the same peloton they were in!

At the same time, racing in Colorado up to altitudes of 13,000 ft, allowed many of these countries' riders time to adapt to the benefits of altitude.

I was selected to compete for the Springbok Road Team in the world championships in Sint-Niklaas, Belgium, in Aug 1984. The team, consisted of Pierre Smit, Willie Engelbrecht, Robbie de Villiers, Bruce Reyneke, Allan Wolhuter and Rudolph Malan. Willie Engelbrecht came 5th, myself 8th and Bruce Reyneke 9th. My experience of this SA team was typical of South African racing up to that point: individuals racing to justify their inclusion in a Springbok team combined with a lack of strategic leadership by the management of the team. Through events like these and teams that were selected for the Rapport Tours, I decided that in future, where possible, I shall put teams together that fit together and can produce the results. Sometimes there are too many Indians and no chiefs. Cyclists do not only consist out of legs but should have hearts and brains too.

1985

By 1985 I started my compulsory National military service. I had the privilege to do my sport during this period. Having knowledge of the European scene and having built valuable contacts in Belgium and Holland, I sought the opportunity for young riders to race overseas and expand their horizons. I discussed this possibility with Defence Force Cycling and they were open to it if the riders cover their own expenses. Obviously, you could not select the best riders, only those that had the means to pay for their trip. I did my best to get the best results out of the riders I had before leaving SA. It was important for them as individuals, the Defence Force and SA cycling.

1985 SADF cycling team to Europe.
Fltr: Wynand Swart, Kobus Oosthuizen, Carl Smith, Francois Retief, Wimpie vd Merwe, Derek Coetzer (sponsor).

In 1985 I took a very inexperienced 5-man team with me, consisting of Francois Retief, Kobus Oosthuizen, Carl Smith and Wynand Swart. We achieved podiums in the minor races, but the main event was the World championship.

The day before the event I received a call from the military attaché in Brussels to inform me that my father died and whether I wanted to return to SA? I just could not desert my team. I was between a rock and a hard place. This was the beginning of our tour and I owed it to persons who depended on me. I decided to stay and support my riders. It was not always easy during this month to pretend that everything was plain sailing because when I phoned home, I was informed that he committed suicide and I did not know the underlying circumstances until later.

My wife was expecting our firstborn within 6 weeks and I wanted to dedicate a win to this event. My team was not strong enough to be of any support. For them, just competing in the event was already a major occurrence. I had enough international racing experience to read the correct breaks and was confident enough to initiate them. Flat road, high-speed racing, suited me. The more difficult the conditions, the better.

In the race, I initiated a break with 13 men and we created a substantial lead. Three quarters into the race I punctured a front wheel and there was no following support vehicle with us at that time. I was standing next to a road filled with thousands of spectators and you could sense the disappointment from the crowd due to my misfortune.

I was waiting more than a minute and still, there was no support vehicle. Out of the crowd came a cyclist with the front wheel of his bicycle in his hand, swopping his for mine. I was grateful and at the same time amazed at the generosity of their cycling public. The next day the rider arrived at the inn we were staying with the wheel and the tyre repaired. He was the mechanic of a local pro team and invited us for a bike set-up and bike check at his place.

When I got back in the race, I was well behind the leading group and well in front of the following peloton. I could not regain my position in the front group and ended in no-man's land in 14th position.

1986

In 1986 I was busy with my second year of national service. The Defence Force Cycling was open to the suggestion of increasing the depth and experience of SADF and SA cyclists through tours that I led overseas. Here was the rationale. If you race every race available in your province in SA it would mean you can participate in a race per weekend. The road season comprised of 6 months, effectively giving you on average 26 road races a year. In the area we stayed in Flanders, you had more than that in total per day to choose from! Should you race daily whilst overseas, you get a year's cycling experience in a month. It just made sense to develop SA riders and fast track them to international and a higher level of cycling than at home.

We had a team put together to compete in the World Championships again. This time it would be held in Belgium in the town of Nazareth. The 6-man team was Anthony Martini, Carlton Willetts, Rian Kuhn, Marcel Reynecke and Lourens Smith. This was a good team. Anthony Martini (RIP), Lourens Smith and Marcel Reynecke were Springbok and junior-Springboks respectively. The other riders represented at provincial level.

Anthony came 3rd in the Rapport Tour and Lourens Smith won it in 1989. Our main focus for the tour was to win the World Championships and to do well in the international multi-day tours we were invited to participate in.

1986 SADF team to Europe.
Fltr front: Anthony Martini, Lourens Smith, Wimpie van der Merwe
Back: Riaan Kuhn, Carlton Willetts, Marcel Reyneke.

The championship route of 150 km was covered 7 times, giving the cycling public a chance to see the riders more than once. The weather on the day was volatile, more than the typical drizzle. The race ended with a proper downpour. This is a race that I should have won.

Throughout my career, I found hidden reserves for the important races. When I escaped, I could stay away and by doing it early I leave the chasing peloton in doubt whether this is a serious matter that should be dealt with immediately or is it a chance to tire a contender? I escaped in the second half of the race and built a lead on my own.

Unfortunately, as a team, we did not have the luxury of a following team car and had to depend on the neutral support vehicle that was supposed to service the whole peloton. I punctured with 6 km to go to the finish and had to wait next to the road for about 2-3 minutes. This cost me the victory.

Motorbike marshals radioed the support vehicle, which was following the second group, which contained the previous year's winner, Cor Verplaencke, Anthony Martini and the eventual winner Pierrot Cuypers. I got my wheel and joined the other 6 riders. The cloud burst started and made riding difficult. Water and cobbles don't mix. You never know if the puddle you race through is a splash of water or a piece of missing pavé. The spray from the rider in front blinded you, so you had to be careful.

1986 World championship in Nazareth, Belgium. 1st Pierrot Cuypers, 2nd Wimpie vd Merwe, 3rd Marnix Verhoye.

Vice prime minister's trophy for the first foreign rider awarded to Wimpie vd Merwe.

The race was to be decided with a sprint. I did not know the other riders in the peloton, only Cor Verplaencke, the current world champion. I knew him from the Rapport Tour and the previous year's races. For me, he was the man to watch. As anticipated, he initiated the sprint early and there was a hesitation from the others to chase. I could not afford cat and mouse for lower placings, so I went after him, caught him, but catapulted the eventual winner, Cuypers, who was on my wheel, to the front. Marnix Verhoye was third and Anthony Martini, fourth.

Bok cyclist second in Belgium

By JAN de KONING

SPRINGBOK Wimpie van der Merwe finished second in the World cycling championships for free amateurs in Belgium yesterday, only one second down on the winner Pirrot Cuypers from Belgium.

Van der Merwe is a member of the Defence cycling team which left for a tour of Belgium recently. They completed in several one day races and will also compete in a stage race.

The world championships, organised by the breakaway group the WAOD, attracted 165 entries and was run over 143 km.

Van der Merwe was in a leading group of cyclists that included fellow Defence and Springbok rider Anthony Martini. Martini finished fifth, only two seconds down on Van der Merwe.

The other Defence riders were equally impressive and all but two finished among the top 15. Carlton Willots 39th and Marcell Reyneke, who could not finish because of an accident he was involved in, is the only two who did not finish among the leaders.

Reyneke was not seriously injured. He got up after he fell but could not catch the bunch again and had to give up.

Results: 1 Pirrot Cuypers (Belgium) 3 hours 23 min; 2 Wimpie van der Merwe (SA) 3:23,01; 3 Marmix Verrooye (Belgium) 3:23,02.
Other South Africans: 5 Anthony Martini 3:23,03 sec; 9 Lourens Smith 3:24,01; 13 Riaan Kuhn 3:24,11; 39 Carlton Willots (no time) and Marcel Reyneke (did not finish.)

Being second was frustrating, not because I was beaten into second, but because of a mechanical, that should have been tended to properly when it occurred. I was content and grateful. For the team, it was a fantastic result. At the time it was one of the best placings for a South African rider in a world championship. It gave them confidence for the multi-day tours that we were to participate in for the next couple of weeks.

The Defence Force and SA were proud. We received extensive coverage in the local press and this caused an embarrassment for the Belgian (BENELUX) embassy in SA. When I reapplied for a visa the following year, this was mentioned. A condition for the following year's visa was that I, Wimpie van der Merwe, could not race, since I was racing on a tourist visa. Our hosts were feeling the heat from the publicity generated by successful SA sportsmen.

1987

By 1987 I was a permanent Defence Force member and at the beginning of my prime. The rules within the Defence Force were that you cannot do professional sport. If you do, you do it in your own time and at your own expense. Turning professional was not an option. The only way for me to reach my potential was through international racing exposure.

My commanding officer, Brigadier Ferdi van Wyk, cornered me one morning, 6 stories below ground level in a nuclear blast-resistant bunker, where we had our offices, and over a cup of coffee, had one of the most important discussions with me that directed my sporting career. He knew of my aspirations to compete in the world champs again and that I was second the previous year due to mechanical misfortune and not because I was beaten into second place. He put a proposition on the table and laid out the scenario to me that SA was in at that moment.

SA was fighting a war against Russian proxies in Angola and on the border of Namibia. We were the dregs of the international community. Our image abroad was bad. We needed positive exposure. Would it be possible, if the Defence Force gives me carte blanche to select a team of my own, that we could win the world championship and other international tours on the European calendar? I immediately said yes, because I knew deep within me the hunger and burning of South Africans to perform overseas. I was assured they would give their 110%.

Brigadier van Wyk registered a project, authorised by the head of the Army, giving me full authority to command whatever unit in the Force to comply. I made a list of all possible candidates in the Defence Force who could cycle and be available for such an undertaking. I understood that since this was more than a cycling tour but an image-building tour of SA, the participants had to be selected carefully. Not all 'who had the legs' were ambassadors and not all who had the psychological capacity to fulfil the role of ambassador were necessarily good cyclists. I had to get a good idea of my 'recruits', what their weak and strong points were.

1987 World champion WAOD – Assenede Belgium.

I had about 6 weeks before the European tour started. I called up all 40+ candidates to Pretoria to be tested by Defence Force psychologists. I tasked the psychologists to develop a battery of tests to determine the psychological skill-set of the profile of the cyclist I was looking for. The profile consisted broadly of traits of being able to work together in a team (normally there were too many chiefs and no Indians), to work under stres and have good ambassadorial skills. When the tests were completed, the psychologists presented me with the results.

I was in a precarious position. My A-team riders, those who had excellent racing results, who had the legs, were nowhere on top of the list. It was the 'B team' category riders that fulfilled the profile I set. These were riders that at best were good club riders, but to be able to perform at an international level, very doubtful. Was I to stick to my instincts of selecting an 'ambassadorial team' or a team based on past performance? I mulled with this for a day or two and decided I shall stick to my guns and select the team that would fulfil the role for which they were meant to be chosen, representing SA and showing the world SA's best side.

The team consisted of myself, Mark Pinder, René Duiker, Paul van Zyl (RIP), Mike Zeeman, Grant Lottering, Martin Saunders and Michael Lagus. These were all national servicemen that would accompany me to Europe to win SA a world championship title. I drafted two men from the SABC for a camp to act as TV crew for the world champs and to report back. This group was led by Nico van Burick.

The last time SA had a cycling world champion on the road was when Laurens Meintjes became the first world cycling champion in 1893. We were scheduled for a 6-week tour, racing in one day and stage race events. The Springbok team would be in Belgium at the same time but for a shorter duration.

The world champs would be our first race. The team was to be thrown into the deep end right from the start of the tour. I used my knowledge of European racing and the way the race could pan out to brief my riders. I explained that they should NOT attack from the word go, but to conserve energy for as long as possible because the contenders would appear in the latter half of the race. They needed to stay out of the fray of things by being close enough to the front to see when escapes occur. The roads were narrow and winding and with 104 riders in the bunch, the peloton could spread out the best part of half a kilometre when the racing is flat out. If the bunch snaps you are in serious trouble and if you aren't in the front, you won't know someone is away. Another fellow South African rider, Francois Otto, was already racing in Europe and he competed in the championship too, but was not part of the team and its strategy.

The ± 150 km race was to be ridden on a course of about 11 km, which crisscrossed into Belgium and the Netherlands and which had sections of cobbles. The streets were lined with people all along the course.

Possibly due to the greatness of the moment and an adrenalin rush, Mark Pinder let loose just after the race got underway. With him was a French rider and Francois Otto. The peloton was playing with them, just keeping them at 30 sec and I realised that my strongest rider was wasting energy and had to come back to the peloton. I bridged the gap to them. That was the last I saw the peloton that day. When I got to them, I summed up the 'energy' and willingness of the participants to make this thing work, because we cannot be dangling in front of the chasing peloton for the rest of the race. We either have to go or return. When the French rider realised that we intended to make the breakaway work and colluded as South Africans, he went to the back and did not want to do any work at the front. He intended to profit from our efforts. After about a dozen attacks from all three of us, he decided it will be an easier ride in the peloton than with us.

We maintained an uncomfortable lead until I suddenly punctured. Was history about to repeat itself? I was already denied two possible world titles through flat tyres. Unfortunately, due to the narrow roads, the service vehicle had not yet joined us, because it was unable to

De Zuidafrikaan Van de Merwe toonde zich iedereen de baas in Assenede.

pass the peloton. The news that I had punctured was conveyed to the following vehicle at the back of the peloton through the spectators on the side of the road.

I made a quality decision that I would ride the flat until I am on to my hub, but I would not be denied again. It was a back-wheel puncture. It was extremely difficult to corner without crashing, but when we hit the first cobbled section it was impossible to continue. I dismounted and waited for the service vehicle, which eventually arrived.

They ripped open the boot and the whole back was full of wheels. I grabbed the first available wheel and when I got underway the peloton was about 200 m behind me. Unfortunately, the chain and cassette were not worn in together. Only the 12 teeth sprocket gave me a smooth ride without the chain jumping. Since you have to down-gear in every corner to accelerate I realised that if the peloton catches me my race would be over, because I would be tactically disadvantaged. I had no option; I had to ride that wheel and get the highest speed possible so I could at least generate the revs for a 54x12.

Wereldkampioenschap vrije amateurs WAOD
Wim Van der Merwe 1 bank vooruit

ASSENEDE - Onder een stralende zomerzon en bij een enorme publieke belangstelling bracht de Zuidafrikaan Wim Van der Merwe zondag een huzarenstukje op fietsgebied. Na zijn tweede plaats van vorig jaar bracht hem dat de titel van wereldkampioen vrije amateurs WAOD op.

Voor de zesde editie van het WAOD wereldkampioenschap kwamen 104 renners aan de start. Nochtans waren er 126 ingeschreven. Ofwel hield het mooie zomerweer sommigen weg van het wielergebeuren, ofwel gaven zij zichzelf geen kans tegen een kransje sterke favorieten. Daarbij hoorde alvast de uiteindelijke overwinnaar Van der Merwe. De vice-wereldkampioen van 1986 kreeg de overwinning echter niet op een presentbladje aangeboden.

De Zuidafrikaan Pinder reed trouwens vier ronden alleen voorop. Vanf de vijfde ronde sloten de Zuidafrikanen Ottu en Van der Merwe en de Fransman Duteau bij de leider aan. Eén ronde later werd Duteau door het peloton gepakt.

Verrassend gingen Ottu en Pinder samen als leiders de achtste ronde in. Van der Merwe volgde (na een lekke band) op 300 meter. In minder dan geen tijd remonteerde hij de vluchters en liet hij hen ter plaatse. Vanaf de negende ronde wordt het wedstrijdverhaal bepaald eentonig. De sterk rijdende Van der Merwe liep steeds verder weg van zijn achtervolgers. Dat was ondertussen een groepje van twaalf renners geworden.

Vooral kampioen van België (kategorie B) Erwin Derekeneire deed daarin verwoede pogingen om de vluchter bij te benen. Tevergeefs echter. Hij moest zich zelfs tevreden stellen met een negende plaats. Het waren overigens nog Erwin Minnebo (Sint Laureyns) en Grant Lottering (Zuid-Afrika) die met Van der Merwe op de pui van het gemeentehuis van Assenede voor hun ereplaatsen werden gehuldigd. (eda)

● **Uitslag :** 1. Wim Van der Merwe (Zuid-Afrika); 2. Erwin Minnebo (Sint-Laureins); 3. Grant Lottering (Zuid-Afrika); 4. Polssens P. 5. Courant F. 6. Pinder N. 7. Luyckx F. 8. Smet M. 9. De Rekeneire E. 10. De Mitse A. 11. Bonneel F. 12. Beelaert R.

DENDER - GENT - OOST - WAAS
Zaterd. 11, zond. 12 juli 1987 — NB

De 29-jarige Zuidafrikaanse legeraalmoezenier Wim Van der Merwe werd zondag de nieuwe wereldkampioen vrije amateurs WAOD. Hij won met ruime voorsprong de zeer lastige koers. De zilveren medaille ging naar de Belg Erwin Minnebo. Een andere Zuidafrikaan, Grant Lottering, kreeg brons. (eda)

Van der Merwe (Z.-Afrika) pakt titel
W.K. vrije liefhebbers te Assenede

Het zesde wereldkampioenschap voor vrije amateurs te Assenede mocht rekenen op een internationale belangstelling, want naast een grote groep Europeanen waren er ook grote delegaties uit Zuid-Afrika en Australië op deze titelrit aanwezig. De Zuidafrikanen hadden die lange reis niet voor niets ondernomen, want zij hebben het gebeuren op imposante wijze beheerst. Dit tot grote vreugde van de persmensen van de Zuidafrikaanse televisie, die met een voltallige staf naar Assenede waren neergereisd.

Hun landgenoot Pinder plaatste de eerste serieuze aanval en fietste een maximale voorsprong van 1.10 minuut bijeen. Even verder in de wedstrijd namen zijn vier landgenoten Ottu, Van der Merwe, Pinder en Duyker het commando over. Deze laatste viel vlug af, waarna vooraan ook Van der Merwe met een defect versnellingsapparaat wegviel. Maar hij gaf de moed niet op, kreeg vlug een nieuwe fiets aangereikt en zou zich in de tweede wedstrijdhelft tot de ware smaakmaker van dit kampioenschap ontpoppen. Hij haalde in een minimum van tijd zijn twee landgenoten bij, waarna hij onmiddellijk met succes demarreerde. Het talrijk opgekomen publiek had zijn sympathie gestolen en steunde hem voluit in zijn succesvolle ontsnapping.

In de achtergrond was een hergroepering tot stand gekomen, waar de ploegmakkers van Van der Merwe oordeelkundig afstopten en niemand in de achtervolging lieten vertrekken.

Bij de aankomst had de nieuwe wereldkampioen bijna 3 minuten voorsprong op Erwin Minnebo uit Sint-Laureins, die zich van een sterk verbrokkelde groep had weten los te maken. De Zuidafrikaan Lotterin werd derde, Roger Beelaerts vierde, Pinder vijfde en Freddy Luyckx eindigde als derde Belg op de zesde plaats. Wim Van der Merwe eindigde vorig jaar achter onze landgenoot Pierrot Cuypers als tweede. Pierrot Cuypers die dit jaar de grote afwezige was.

J.B.

I passed Mark Pinder and Francois Otto after a short while, but they could not latch on. I was desperate that the peloton should not catch me. I ran out of carry-on provisions as well as water. Paul van Zyl abandoned the race by then and he made his carry-on supplies available to me from the side of the road. We had the SA TV/film crew filming me from a motorcycle. We had so much faith in the success of our venture that we brought them along!

1987 World champion WAOD – Assenede Belgium. *Receiving the awards at the prize giving.*

I won the race with a 3 min lead, the largest gap for a leader to win the race by. Erwin Minnebo was second and fellow teammate, Grant Lottering, third. Grant would eventually become a pro rider in SA. Our team was so proud. We came as underdogs and outperformed the best.

In the following weeks, we participated in international tours, in which the Springbok team participated too. Our Defence Force 'B Team' was so pumped up that we won all the multi-day tours we raced in, beating the Springboks in all the races that we were competing in together to the dismay of Gotty Hansen and brigadier Combrinck, their managers. It proved my instinct to choose riders that rally around a common purpose, rather than to select individuals that each wanted to justify his inclusion in a team. We were beating countries like Germany, Italy, France, Belgium and SA.

Immediately after the championship, I had a call from France, from René Gautier, chairman from a club in Normandy, inviting me to race there. I declined the invitation unless they invited my team and our entourage with me. The next day a massive tour bus arrived at Heidebloem and whisked us away to France. We were put up in a hotel and we raced in Normandy for a week, being carried on the hands by the French cycling public. This European tour laid the groundwork for bigger things to come for individuals in our team who went on to become Springboks and negotiate pro contracts.

The full extent of SA having a world champion was not promoted in SA, except by the international media and our Defence Force. The team was honoured by the head of the Defence Force and Minister of Defence, congratulating us on what was accomplished.

Before I went to the world championship my SA licence was revoked by the SACF, because I had a sponsor from a Namibian company to compete in a Namibian team triathlon later in the year. The SACF felt that part of the money should come to them, as declared by the SACF sponsorship rules because I was a South African cyclist and under their jurisdiction. Because this sponsorship was not declared to them, though it being a completely different sports discipline and participation in a different country, they withdrew my cycling licence.

I was thus no more a SA cyclist and for that matter, whatever I do from then on I could not break any of their rules. Had they suspended me, I would have been a licenced rider without privileges as long as the suspension lasted. This was a tactical mistake on their side because now they could not prevent me from competing overseas in the world championships. I thus had to apply for a Belgian racing licence to compete (as the rest of our team did).

When Gotty Hansen, Springbok manager, 'congratulated' me after the race, he made the remark that I won the race on purpose to spite them (sic).

Normally a cycling federation would make a whoo-hah and beat the drums if they had a champion in their ranks, but since I was their persona non-grata this team was by association too. Up to this day the Cycling Federation has never acknowledged or congratulated me on this victory, though the whole world did. Our team left SA as a Defence Force B Team and after beating the Springboks in every race as well as other national teams, we left egg on their faces.

The 1987 SADF team to Europe & supporters
Fltr front: Wimpie & Christa vd Merwe with Chris, Mike Lagus, Mike Zeeman, Paul van Zyl & wife. Middle: Mark Pinder, Belgian supporter, Martin Saunders, Philip Smet and friend (Belgian supporters), Erwin Minnebo and wife (silver medal).
Back: René Duiker, Grant Lottering (bronze medal).

What we accomplished then has never officially been honoured in the old dispensation. Very few know of this underdog team's accomplishment, having made South Africa proud. The overseas publicity was immense, so much so that I was again officially reprimanded by the Belgian embassy in SA, advising me not to apply for another visa, since I was blacklisted for circumventing the sports boycott. They had no problem with allowing us to participate in sport and keeping it under the radar, but we have broken the sound barrier with this tour and have embarrassed them.

I recognise and honour my fellow riders who succeeded in doing a job exceedingly well, who never really received the honour as soldiers who fought in an asymmetrical war of counter-propaganda and succeeded brilliantly. They would agree, however, that they, as I, enjoyed every moment of it!

In 1993, in preparation for the International Human Powered Vehicle Speed Championship (IHPVSC) in America, I went to Belgium to prepare. On one of my training rides, I decided to revisit Assenede, the battleground of my victory 6 years before.

As I was travelling down the busy main road of the town a pedestrian jumped off the pavement into the road, shouting, 'Wim van der Merwe, Wim van der Merwe!' I was utterly surprised and stunned that someone would recognise me in a town I have visited only once before and then was camouflaged by a helmet and big Oakley glasses that covered half my face! It showed me how serious the cycling public in Europe take their sport and how closely they identify with their heroes as supporters. I stopped and found out that I signed a SA flag for him that I handed out to well-wishers.

1993

IHPVSC WORLD CHAMPIONSHIPS

The 19th International Human Powered Speed Championships were held in Minneapolis, USA in 1993. The venue was in Blaine, Minnesota. The road and track events were hosted there. I was invited to participate. By then I was a multiple world record holder in this discipline. The records I held were over distances ranging from 4 km – 24 hours.

I organised TV cameraman, Fred Phyfer and manager, Eddie Kriel to accompany me. I intended a month-long trip, with the first half being in Belgium, preparing and sharpening myself for the world championships by participating in the local races. In my first race in Belgium, I hit a pothole on the cobbles and snapped the frame in three. I injured my thighs by bruising them badly. The intent of racing now changed to the intent of recuperating in time for the world championships. I used most of the days to mend that what was injured by riding long distances slowly. This helped.

We left for America and Fred was to join us later. He had separate filming commitments for the SABC in New York. Eddie and I arrived in Minneapolis in the middle of the night. We had to travel from there to Blaine where the velodrome was and the championships would be held. It was about an hour's drive from the airport. The only problem was that it was in the middle of the night with no car services or any transport services available to transport us and a big crated bicycle. It was not a good start.

Fltr: Eddie Kriel, Fred Phyfer and Wimpie vd Merwe at Schipol airport enroute to the world championships in Minneapolis.

1993 International Human Powered Speed Championship in the USA. The Spirit of Engen at over 80 km/h in the banking of the velodrome.

Things happen smoothly, slipping out the hands of Eddie Kriel in a drag-race start.

Our fortunes changed when a guy who was on the same flight, with a wide-brimmed Texan Stetson hat, offered to take us to Blaine. We were soon exposed to American hospitality.

The next day we collected the crate and could start with test runs on the track. The track was an intimidating 43-degree, 250 m outdoor, wooden track. At 80 km/h the G-forces were tremendous. It was the first time I rode a 250 m track and which was as steeply angled as that. My trials were to ride the black line. When in the curve or corner of the track, looking through the cockpit window that black line appeared as a straight line directly in front of you and upwards. You could only see 10 m ahead of you. This changed once you hit the straight for a couple of seconds and then you were back into the vision of the 'wall of death'.

The concern was that if you catch up with a slow rider in front of you, as in the 4 km individual pursuit, you could be crashing full speed into him because you would not have ample warning that you are overtaking. These were some of the risks I was taking and I needed to prepare myself mentally for this.

I got a call from Fred Phyfer, whilst in Blaine, informing me that he was robbed in New York of his R250,000 (1993 value!) TV camera. This left us in a great predicament as the agreement of our sponsorship with our sponsors was TV coverage. We had to rent a camera in America for the duration of the championships.

For an important championship, you normally select a few speciality events to compete in. However, SA was just readmitted to international sport the year before and there was a great hunger to participate against the world, so I entered all the events. This created problems for the organisers as heats in different events were following one after the other

Transporting the HPV internationally on a shoe string budget was challenging. Between myself, Eddie Kriel and Fred Phyfer (TV camera man) we managed the seemingly impossible.

and with a rider, as myself, progressing through the quarter and semi-finals, it became more difficult to organise the flow as I was participating in the finals of most of the events.

The events ranged from road to track. I had to ride my bike between events from venue to venue, e.g., the sprints and drag racing were held on the tarmac of the local airfield, supplying a long enough track for these events. Then you had to speed over to the velodrome a couple of km away to participate in a heat over there and then over to the circuit in town for the criterium road event.

A harvest of 7 gold and 4 silver medals at the HPV world championships in 1993 in the USA.

When your desire to participate is high these are experienced as minor disturbances. Of the 14 events, I eventually won 7 gold and 4 silver.

Some memorable events of the championships were not on the track or bike, but on how we managed an event of this proportion on a shoestring budget. We stayed in the sport's hostel at the Velodrome. Most of the athletes and entourage were housed there, like an Olympic village. We had to feed ourselves, however.

To be able to do this, especially when cyclists consume food to finance their high caloric expenditure, you had to find places in town with specials on food. You needed to know which place had the deal to eat as much as you can for the same price and on which day. Most of these were pizza establishments. After a week you could become quite averse, at looking a pizza in the eye. You knew you were on the special for the day when the crust is wider than the topping. So, when British rider, Jonathan Wooldrich, offered us a lift in his van to eat out in another neighbourhood at a restaurant that served meat, we accepted very enthusiastically.

Our eyes scanned for the specials, the eat-as-much-as-you-can ones. We found one, the bottomless ribs. In SA eating ribs are not a challenge, since it is more bones than meat. When our plates arrived, we had steaks on the plate as big as shoe soles and as thick as Encyclopaedia Britannica. The 'steak' was the meat cut off from the rib and no bones formed part of the deal. This was fantastic news. Boneless ribs. It sounded something like heatless fire, but who cared? When I ordered my seventh portion a message was sent from the kitchen from the chef, thanking me that I was enjoying his ribs and proudly announcing that I have just broken the record.

It was rumoured the next day, that the word that went round among the riders at the championships, was that if you want to ride like Wimpie you had to eat like Wimpie!

9. THE RUNNER

IN 1987 AFTER winning the world championships in Europe I could not continue cycling in SA as I had no licence, it was revoked by the SACF. During the early 80's I competed in a series of track events where combined athletics and cycling events were held on the same evening. This helped me build good relationships in the athletics scene amongst some of the top athletes. Knowing top cyclists helped them when they needed cyclists for team triathlons.

Run-Cycle Duathlons was a fledgeling sport in 1988, birthing from out of Triathlon and the Swim-Run Duathlons. The greatest exposure cyclists had to triathlons were by competing in team events where each leg of the triathlon was done by a specialist. This would be either swimming or canoeing, running and then cycling. The top cyclists were known among those who put these teams together and the cyclists were regularly called upon to represent sponsored teams.

I thus competed in several team triathlons in SA and Namibia. The team triathlons were good for the development of Duathlons because participants of various disciplines could 'look over the fence' and see who was participating and what they were doing. This encouraged a person to try out a discipline on the other side of the fence, as was the case with me, trying out running.

For the first time, Duathlon events were held in Northern Transvaal and I was the first pure cyclist to participate. The rest were mostly triathletes and runners.

For my first Duathlon Piet Maré, Springbok canoeist, loaned me his shoes, as we had the same size feet. I had no running shoes. I think I did the fastest leg for the cycling but just average in the running. I realized this was a completely different animal. The following days I was as stiff as a stick.

I needed proper running shoes and went to the shoe company, Onitsuka Tiger, in Centurion and applied for a shoe sponsorship. They fitted me out with kit, shoes and much more. By then Johan Fourie, Springbok middle-distance runner, started participating in Duathlons too. He appeared at the one race, shortly afterwards, with a brand new sponsored Alpina bicycle. Surprised I asked him how did he manage that, because I, as a cyclist, cannot even get that kind of sponsorship. He looked at my shoes and asked, how did you get that shoe sponsorship? I, as a runner, can't get that. Ironic!

Various team triathlons and duathlon medals.

DUATHLONS

I had no running muscle memory or muscle development for running. I had to start as a beginner. I had cardiovascular fitness and possibly less running damage compared to someone of my size would have had, who had been running for years. I initially picked up the typical overuse problems of the IT band but was soon able to maintain a 3:30 min/km pace in the running leg of the duathlons, which normally consisted of a 10 km run and then a 30-40 km time trial with the bike.

The exponents were Glen Gore in the seniors and Harold Zumpt in the junior division. Johan Fourie and I were always breathing in each other's necks. The shorter the cycling leg was the more it benefitted the runner. In 1988 I received my Northern Transvaal colours and came 4th in the SA championships, just behind Johan Fourie. In 1990 Springbok colours were awarded, but with my moving down to the Cape in September 1989 and Duathlon still being very non-existent there, there were no real opportunities to compete and assure a place in this team. My love and interest were in cycling and not running, so this venture as a competition died due to a lack of interest. However, staying on a wine farm in the Stellenbosch district enabled me to run with my dog daily in the surrounding mountains and vineyards.

THE COMRADES

Whilst on the Namibia and Angola border, doing my Border duties, the commanding officer of our base, Elundu, informed us that there was an upcoming marathon in Grootfontein and it was expected of every base to send a contingent of runners. I had to lead from the front and put up my hand as a volunteer.

How do you train for an event like this in a low-intensity war zone? You did not come to the Border with running gear like running shorts or shoes, etc. There were only two options for me. The sappers went out daily to sweep the roads for mines. They cover up to 40 km a day with metal detectors with a following Buffel, a mine-resistant vehicle, carrying the team of sappers who relay one another so the distance could be covered in a day. I thought I could walk behind the Buffel so that I at least get hours in the legs.

Big was my surprise when I went out for this mine sweeping exercise on how they do it. I suppose the sappers became specialists in observing tell-tale signs for the planting of a mine on a road. There was no walking the distance with metal detectors. Two sappers were sitting on the front of the Buffel looking down at the road for disturbances in the dirt whilst the others were looking out for a terrorist ambush. I only went out one day with them and realised if I cannot run at 40 km/h I shall not be able to use this as training. I had to look for an alternative.

At my base Elundu, about 100 m of the bush was cleared around it so that, in case of an attack, you had this as a killing ground. The Namibian border is typically white soft sand, making it easy to track someone and difficult to move fast on foot. This was the ideal training ground for me, running around the base in this sand. The only shoes I had for this were my army boots, making it a good handicap for the time spent running.

My son, at the time, was 2 years old and any army paraphernalia were collectables to him, things like the fins of mortars and shells of spent ammunition. On this particular run, as I was in the killing zone, I observed the fins of a mortar sticking out of the ground. Most of the mortars I picked up were the back half of mortar flares, shot off during an attack to illuminate the area. This was particularly large fins and I was pleased with the find. I stopped to pick it up, but as I pulled on it, it did not want to come out. I started digging it out and realised it was a live round that did not detonate and might explode if the front part was lifted.

I reported this and the next day we were treated to a big bang and fireworks display when the neighbouring base brought in all their expired helicopter ammunition, placed it on the live mortar and detonated it. Everyone in the base was informed and with the needed alarm we kept our heads and bodies out of harm's way in the surrounding bunkers.

Shortly after, the medics rushed to the doctor's tent, more than 600 m away from the blast when some of the shrapnel hit a patient standing in the queue, waiting for medical treatment. All of this drama just by running around in the sand, around a base!

Eventually, the day of the marathon arrived and the couple of us going to run the marathon were loaded onto a SAMIL and transported to Grootfontein, which took us a couple of hours to get there. I was issued with the standard 'running shoe' of the Army, khaki coloured tennis shoes. It was so high tech I could just as well have run barefoot.

The run was dominated by pure racing snakes. I stayed with them possibly for the first four or five km, when I told myself to take it easy. I have never run further than 21 km and I was running at a pace that I have never run before.

At the water points, you got exactly that, water. There were no fancy drinks, no energy replacement. It was turning out a very crude race, very Spartan and typically army. When I reached the 32 km water point, I stopped for the first time to drink my water, whilst standing still. The most bizarre thing happened, I could not put one foot before the other. I went into rigor mortis and could not continue. I was loaded onto the SAMIL, following as the broom wagon, like a pole.

For the next week, I was placed on extreme light duty. Luckily there were no stairs in the base or else it would have been an embarrassment to have been carried up and down. Bending my knees, just to sit on a toilet was agonizing. This was my humble experience of marathon running.

In March 2000 one of our friends in the Strand Athletics club, Elma du Plessis, challenged me to run the Comrades marathon. I am a person that is ready for challenges, especially if they are of the extreme and endurance kind. I wanted to know how do I go about it? She said that one had to qualify by running a marathon in a certain minimum time. The last and geographically closest qualifying marathon before the Comrades was the Cape Town marathon, happening that weekend. If I don't use the opportunity, I shall have to travel to up-country events to qualify.

I have never completed a marathon before. I had this terrible experience with my first attempt and I was still humbled that I was a DNF. The challenge to me was that never did a cyclist with international achievements, at that time, ever run the Comrades. It would be a first if I can do it. I did not have running shoes. I only had fashionable sneakers. At least I knew how to spread my energy over a few hours of activity.

My first marathon entered on the spur of the moment with a day licence, running with Elma du Plessis in the Cape Town marathon in 2000.

Elma said she was aiming at a 3:30 marathon. That made no sense to me. I did not know if that was fast or slow, whether she was warning me or trying to encourage me with a slowish time. I decided that I shall use her as a pacer and see if the pace matches my ability. I entered the marathon with a day licence and with some apprehension. I am the kind of guy that doesn't allow women to beat me in the same event. So, a little bit of male pride and shielding of my male ego was at stake when the gun went off in Cape Town at 06:00 that morning.

I am not a light person, so running does not come naturally to me unless a dog or police chase me, then it becomes very naturally! Up to about 3 hours of running, I matched Elma stride for stride, but then the lack of proper running shoes took its toll. My knees were all over the place. Eventually, it felt as if I was running on stumps. The pain and discomfort were terrible. I finished in 3:35 but went into immediate rigor mortis as I crossed the line.

Where I stopped and laid down, I had to be dragged away, because I could not bend a leg. I could not even get into my car at UCT to drive home. For the next week, I was as stiff as a pole.

After I recovered from the rigor mortis, I went to buy myself some proper running shoes. I spoke to Bruce Fordyce. He made some suggestions about brands and whether they should be supination or pronation shoes. At the one store, I was helped by a proper runner. He made some suggestions and ended with the following, 'go out and test the shoes. If they don't suit you bring them back and try something else. Do about 10 km, but keep to the tar road so we can pack them back into the box if you don't want them.' I was horrified. Knowing how far 10 km was, it was no joke to me. Did he want me to do the 10 km in stages? That was just to see if the shoes fit! I thought he was out of his mind.

Six weeks after the CPT Marathon was the Two Oceans 56 km marathon. Since I was now in the running business, I should at least sharpen my teeth on the 'shorter' events, before tackling the long one. My training comprised more resting than running because I was becoming stiff after every run and had to rest enough just to be able to walk again. By now I was a licenced runner and entered for the Two Oceans.

That morning, on Easter Saturday, we started in Wynberg Main Road and after 4 km into the run, I heard this terrible sound like a tent zip being opened or closed and then this burning sensation in my left buttock. I tore my Gluteus. I ran like a person stricken with polio or some form of ambulatory disability. At first, I did not know what happened. I just knew I had pain and was running like a drunk person. I realized that if I quit, I shall not run again. I decided to grit my teeth and complete the event, which I did, five and a half hours later.

It was later diagnosed that the problem was underdeveloped support muscles on the side of my hips, due to years of cycling, and thus not supplying support for the hip movement that occurs naturally when running.

Eventually, I ended up only running Marathons. My best time was 3:05. Half marathons were 'too short'. I completed 4 Two Oceans and finished 5 Comrades Marathons, all of them

4 Two Oceans medals.

5 Bill Rowan Comrades medals.

Bill Rowan medals (sub 9 hrs). I missed silver in my last Comrades in 2004 with about 10 minutes.

You cannot run the Comrades distance of 88 km to train for the Comrades. It takes many runners about a month to recuperate. I regularly ran 40 km at times with my dog, Laika. She was a German shepherd cross with a Labrador. She was the fittest dog in town. I started running with her at the age of six weeks, training her to run on my side, away from the traffic. She knew the routes I had. I had to plan the route to pass farm dams regularly so that she could drink water and cool down. A Labrador is a water dog, so she just enjoyed being in the water. She had long white hair from her Alsatian mother, which made her uncomfortably hot. She had to cool herself down by jumping into the dams we pass.

On this particular route in Somerset West, we pass a fenceless house and the people had a pool or Khoi pond at their front door. Every time we pass there she rushes ahead, jumps in the pond, drinks water, splashes around and after I passed, jumped out and rushed back. As I pass this house, I had to keep the pose of: 'I don't know that dog. That dog is not mine, however, I can call him for you so you can stop screaming at him to get out of your pool. Doggy, doggy!'

If I used the word 'run' or touched my running shoes she went berserk. She knew all the ruffian dogs in the neighbourhood. When we passed those properties, she would run down the length of the fence and make an abrupt about-turn, causing the dogs, chasing her, to run into one another when she turned. They were caught every time and she enjoyed it. She knew where the trees with the squirrels were and loved chasing them to and up the trees. Together we had great fun preparing for the long runs. My dog became my training partner and shadow.

Somehow the action of running acted as an enema on me. It did not matter whether I have been to the toilet just before I started, but after 40 minutes I had to go again. This happened to me in the races too. The up Comrades brought me to Pinetown within this critical 40 minutes after starting. Along the route blue mobile toilets were stationed for the runners. When we reached the first ones there were already queues of people at each one of them, mostly the public. I realised there would be no toilet booth for me and decided to look for the thickest shrub on the sidewalk.

Pinetown has wide sidewalks. The crowds were standing on the curb about five, six deep, cheering the runners on. Behind them, you have the shrubbery and then the sidewalk lane next to the houses' fences. When you have to go you have to go. There were no inhibitions left. I pulled down my pants and got on my haunches and answered mother nature's call when a woman came running through the bushes and sat a metre away from me, doing the same! What could I do? There was no time to feel embarrassed or go through the formalities of introducing oneself. Slowly, but cautiously I covered my race number on my chest. I did not want to be identified! Her face, however, is still imprinted in my memory...

In a way, I enjoy being a male chauvinist, someone who walks on the traffic side of a lady when on the sidewalk, allowing the lady to enter a door first, opening doors for them, etc. I thus do not mind being called chauvinist. It will be a badge of honour. In this way, I grew up that the lady is the weaker sex and the male is there to protect and care for her.

I had a rude awakening on my first Comrades. At about 65 km, there is this little man that jumps out from the bushes and hits you with a hammer on your knees. You can't prevent it from happening. For others, on the up run, he appears at Polly Shorts, 10 km from the finish.

As this little man was continuously hitting me with the hammer on the knees it felt as if I was running on bleeding stumps. I was using all my inner strength and self-talk to remind myself that all are feeling the same pain. I tried to convince myself that feeling pain is a sign I am still alive. I motivated myself by telling myself that there were some people today that prayed for legs and would give anything to experience the pain that I was feeling.

Then suddenly! From a distance behind me, I could hear two women chatting to one another. The topics changing from problems with the kiddies and the latest recipe they ought to try out. Two ladies were closing in on me and were about to pass me. My male ego responded, 'pull back the shoulders, lift the knees and stay in front of them. No woman ought to be running faster than you.'

I just could not accelerate. They passed me. My shoulders slumped and I got back into the Comrades shuffle. My eyes could not believe what I was seeing as they passed me, two fat women, with hail damage on their thighs, running faster than what I was running! They eventually finished ahead of me. I finished in the first 1,000 of the more than 12,000 that

started the day. Never underestimate a woman. I make the observation that everyone goes crazy about people doping with testosterone, but what about oestrogen? This is giving them the edge!

Everyone who was a newbie to the discipline of running had to read Tim Noakes' 'Lore of Running', the bible of distance running. I did and it prepared me well. You attended whatever informative talk you could 'to know the enemy'. Still, nothing prepares you for the pain and discomfort. On the down run, normally doing the most damage to the legs, you have a giggle the next morning on the beachfront in Durban and at the airport. It is as if everyone in Durban tries not to wake up the sleeping pills. Everyone tiptoes and walks very, very slowly.

I preferred the marathon and ultra-distances. The False Bay 50, Two Oceans 56 km and Comrades fitted into this category.

What is amazing about the Comrades is the atmosphere and camaraderie. The majority of runners come in just before the final moments, getting full value for their entry fee. Others, like myself, who challenge themself, squeeze every drop of willpower out to run the best possible time, form the other side of the spectrum. The public encourages both, but I think the back enders draw the most sympathy and loudest cheers.

This has become a cultural event. This is how the Tour de France is supported, becoming a tourist attraction with people coming from abroad, not only for the race but the ambience.

When I broke my back four times already since 2013 the orthopaedic surgeon showed me my scans. I was already 3 cm shorter than the longest I have been. This was due to the impact running had on my body, especially as a heavier person. The cartilage in between the vertebrae in the back compress and with every accumulated millimetre per vertebrae it becomes centimetres over the whole spine. This was my wake-up call.

If I wanted a healthy back in old age I had to stop running and continue with a non-weight bearing exercise, cycling. I had to embrace my first love again.

10. 'VAL & RY' VAN DER MERWE

I WAS DUBBED by Gielie Laing, reporter of Die Burger, and other journalists of the time as 'Ry & Val Van der Merwe' due to the many crashes I were involved in. This could be construed that I did not know how to ride a bike, but it was mostly due to other factors.

Just after breaking the endurance world record of Dries Oberholzer in 1975, one of the reporters of the Transvaler, André Pienaar, asked whether I would want to race in a kermesse in the southern suburbs of Johannesburg? He lent me a brand new, wet look, glossy green cycling jersey for the occasion. I arrived there, bike equipped with clincher tyres, cotter pin cranks and with my sneakers for cycling shoes. A young Alan van Heerden was one of the riders that day and who eventually won the race.

I crashed twice in the same race. The skin was grazed off both my hands. The chairman of the Northern Wheelers Cycling club bandaged me and asked me not to stop racing because of what happened. The brand-new cycling jersey was not so brand new anymore. André Pienaar told me to rather keep it as a souvenir. I started my first race as I was later nicknamed.

In 1977, in my first year of official racing, I was eligible to race my first race on the Cycling Calendar as a licenced rider in the Novice race. I crashed in this race too and in several others in my first year or two. It cost me regularly replacing rims, handlebar tape, clothing and paying for medical treatment.

I later analysed why I was involved in these pile-ups and came to the realization that it was because of poor bike handling by riders crashing in front of me and that I did not want to be the cause of more riders falling so I took the punch by veering out of the way and many times crashing myself. I am too of the opinion that riders overseas, in 'cycling countries' are better at handling their bikes than locally. I have never been involved in any crash outside SA, except in my last race I rode in Europe where my SA manufactured frame snapped in three when I went through a pothole on the cobbles.

Some of my crashes were due to equipment failure. In this particular instance, we were in a Western Province Road race in 1982 where we had to contest a hot spot prime at Elgin, in the Western Cape. It was a slight downhill sprint and the leading contenders were still all together. In this sprint, I had a lead-out and my teammates were on my wheel. As I got out of the saddle to sprint past, I hit the deck. I snapped my crank. Needless to say, it was a slaughterhouse.

My fellow Springbok rider, Pierre Smit, recalled that when he got on his bike, he was so dazed that he started riding in the opposite direction going where he was coming from. My other teammate, Fourie Kotze, was bleeding profusely and was loaded into the following ambulance. He was more concerned about the new Reynolds 753 tubing TI Raleigh bike he had just bought. He wanted to know the condition it was in and its whereabouts. The medics were loading the ambulance from the side door with injured cyclists and every time they put Fourie in he escapes out the back door, looking for his bike.

When I later adopted the saying, 'skin grows back, Campagnolo does not' things started improving. If someone was stupid enough to crash in front of me, I tried to stay upright even if it meant riding over him. None of them was paying my bills. Once I made that cruel decision of every man for himself, I fell less.

Even by making this decision, I was involved in some spectacular and famous crashes, especially on the Rapport Tour as well as other less dramatic ones.

1977 RAPPORT TOUR
In the 1977 Rapport Tour, riding with riders like Eddie King and Alan van Heerden in the same canary yellow outfit of the Solly Kramer team I crashed and fractured my elbow in the first stage. The stage was between Johannesburg and Potchefstroom. About an hour before the stage finished a German rider, in front of me, rode over a stone and crashed and brought me down. With outstretched arms, I tried to break the fall and, in the process, broke the elbow joint.

I got on my bike and pursued the bunch that was disappearing down the road. I did not know the extent of the damage. With one arm clutched against my chest and the other on the handlebars I chased. I could not catch the bunch I was in. The tour doctor came to me

Rapport Tour 1977 – Assisting Eddie King with my broken elbow in a sling after he crashed just before the finish.

immediately on arrival and gave instructions that I should be taken to the hospital for X-rays. There the elbow fracture was confirmed. They put my arm in a cast and released me.

I was ready to race the next day. The doctor and other Tour officials had a chat with me, realizing that this was a great disappointment to me, advised me that I still had a great cycling future ahead of me and should not despair.

This misfortune opened the door for me to ride the Tour in the race director and referee's car for the remainder of the tour, observing tactics and receiving running commentary from persons more knowledgeable than myself about cycling. I gained more experience of cycling from this vantage point than being on the saddle of a bike.

1978 RAPPORT TOUR
I was riding my second Rapport Tour in the Holiday Inn team with the likes of Toney Impey and Ertjies Bezuidenhout. We were riding a route that was taking us from Cape Town via the eastern, coastal parts of the country and Durban to Johannesburg. Riders like Alan van Heerden were seconds overall behind Marco Chagas of Portugal, in yellow. With every stage, Alan gained a couple of seconds overall, edging closer and closer, but Chagas was not a slouch either. He was a Tour de France rider and knew how to defend yellow. We thus knew that if you are on the wheel of either of these two you will be in the best possible position for the sprint.

On the stage finishing into Newcastle, we were preparing for a mass sprint for the line. The wind was from the right and the slip to the left. The lead-out for Chagas was on the right-hand side of the road and Van Heerden shadowing him. I was 4 riders behind Van Heerden with teammate Pieter Kemp in front of me. We entered the last kilometre and the sprint was already flat out.

Suddenly Van Heerden jumped for the left-hand side of the road to deny a slip for any following riders and to surprise Chagas. Unfortunately, he had a whole peloton following, overlapping one another's wheels. Not considering that he could cause a crash, he jumped to the left and took the front wheel out from the rider behind him and that rider the wheel from the rider behind him and so on. In a split second a portion of the bunch went down like dominoes and Van Heerden and the riders who were in front of him were the ones sprinting for the line. Van Heerden won and the bloodied riders on the road got bunch-time because the crash occurred in the final kilometre.

I crashed heavily, having no skin left on the right-hand side of my body. I arrived in Johannesburg a couple of days later still bandaged like a mummy.

1982 RAPPORT TOUR
There were some famous falls I could escape from but in which I was still involved.

The 1982 Tour was from Nelspruit to Cape Town and I was racing for the Springbok team. Alan van Heerden was wearing yellow already early on in the race. We were to finish the stage in Bloemfontein. As with all flat stages, they are always fast and furious. I was in the front of the peloton and launched an attack. Van Heerden was on my wheel. I assume his front wheel overlapped my back wheel when at high speed he came down, bringing down 12 of the peloton. As I looked back, I was nearly the only rider still upright. It was carnage. The back riders had to climb over the pile of bicycles to continue.

Rodney Fowler, a teammate of Van Heerden, who made it through the war zone first, warned me that if I do not wait for Van Heerden, who was at the bottom of the mess, there would be repercussions further on in the race. I just wonder if the same would be true if I was at the bottom of that pile?

Van Heerden sustained a fractured skull with which he continued to win the Tour. He became a familiar sight wearing his daily turban under his strip helmet. Cor Verplaencke, from Belgium, sustained serious head injuries and had to be withdrawn and hospitalised. Many of the riders sported wounds for the rest of the Tour.

1984 RAPPORT TOUR

The 1984 edition of the Rapport Tour went a circular route from Johannesburg to Durban and back to Johannesburg. I was racing for the Imperial Truck Hire team. We were 20 km out from the stage finish in Volksrust when I hit a golfball-sized rock in the road which caused my front wheel to uncouple from the fork and I crashed. This brought down several riders, including Alan Wolhuter.

The next day we were racing down the escarpment into Estcourt when I hit a fist-sized glass cateye in the middle of the road. Nato Barnard, photographer of Rapport was sitting back to front on the passenger seat of the motorbike in front of the group when this happened. He filmed the incident with fast shuttering and you could later analyse how the accident occurred.

When my front wheel hit the cateye it deflected and bent the rim. As the rim passed through the brake callipers it locked, catapulting me over the bars and into the road. The impact crushed my wrist. As I went down my bicycle flew through the air and hit a rider in the

Rapport Tour 1984 – The big crash in Estcourt that left me with a crushed wrist.

DIE groot val ... Wimpie van der Merwe van die Springbokspan het gister naby Pietermaritzburg gedurende die RAPPORT-Toer hard met die teerpad kennis gemaak, soos die foto's duidelik aandui. Sy linkerarm is gebreek en op 'n plek feitlik vergruis. Hy sal môre 'n operasie moet ondergaan en is uit die Toer. Jannie van den Berg is steeds die algehele voorloper van die Toer.

group on the far left. As I was coming down, I heard Allan Wolhuter screaming, 'Not again! Not again!' His wounds of the previous day have not even formed scabs yet when he came slamming over me again at full speed.

The orthopaedic surgeon had to be called from the golf course. He was not happy to interrupt his golf game. All that he asked me was what was my profession? I told him. He said, in that case, I don't need a functional wrist and just set it in a cast. The Tour doctor, Dawie van Velden, was upset and immediately got me on a flight to Cape Town for reconstructive surgery which turned out to be successful.

1885 RAPPORT TOUR
The 13th edition of the Rapport Tour was from Johannesburg to Cape Town. I was riding for the NVVR/NRSC Defence Force team. The Tour was coming for a stage finish into Bloemfontein. It was a flat and very fast stage. We were coming along the N1 highway. The highway had the usual yellow line to demarcate a safety and emergency lane. As cyclists, we were using any legal piece of tar to ride on, especially when there is a gutter wind as in this particular case.

The wind was from the side and the gutter to the left. By going flat out in these conditions you break the peloton at the weak links. As a rider, you don't want a weak link in front of you because then you have to cross that no man's land to try and get some protection from the rider ahead.

In the meanwhile, traffic officials pulled traffic off the road. They made a mistake by pulling cars off the road going the same direction as the riders, instead of letting them pass and get ahead, they made some of them stop on the side.

The peloton was stretched out for more than 100 metres, all on the left-hand side edge of the road. I was on the wheel of Hennie (Wiele) Wentzel. I knew he was not a weak link and decided to stick to him like glue. He is a much smaller rider than I was and therefore did not give much slipstream. I had to get as low as possible. In front of the group of cyclists, a car with a family inside was pulled off the road and was standing in the yellow lane and on the tar. As the cyclists reached the car, they each swerved out as late as possible to delay the benefit of the slipstream they create when they passed it on the right-hand side.

Rapport Tour 1985 – Slamming into the rear of a stationary car just before Bloemfontein.

Wiele timed his passing perfectly because when he swerved to the right to pass, I went straight into the car. Raoul de Villiers, race director, later said, when he saw the accident, he thought the tour was going to have its first fatality. I moved the car ahead with about

2 m. I catapulted and spun through the air. This I achieved by hitting both thighs against the handlebars as my bike crumpled up below me. This sent me cartwheeling through the air. In the meanwhile, teammate Mark Jansen, passed the car on the gravel, on the left, when I dropped like a parabat out of the sky on top of him. This broke my fall. My legs were badly bruised. My team manager got me my spare bike and I pedalled to finish the stage.

ARGUS TOUR (ACT)

We have just built our first back wheel driven human powered vehicle (HPV) from fibreglass and mild steel tubing to compete in the 1991 ACT. We had to test the recumbent on the route of the Argus, the week before the event to see if the gearing was ok for the climbs, that everything was tight and secure and running as it should.

As I went from Smitswinkel's climb around to Misty Cliffs there were some road works on this stretch of road where shallow ditches were dug across the road. The tar had sharp edges. Unlike a normal upright bicycle where you can jump over obstacles, you cannot with a recumbent because you were lying on your back. The bike takes the full impact. In this instance, without me being aware of it, I damaged the tyres.

Whilst at speed of around 70-80 km/h on the downhill to Misty Cliffs I had a blowout on one of the tyres. As I crashed my canopy came loose from the bottom and I became exposed and left a sizable amount of skin on the tar. We learnt a lesson and that was that the top canopy had to be attached to the bottom with Velcro strips on the inside.

For the 1992 ACT, we used the same design but built the fairing with a carbon fibre Kevlar mix for extra safety. The speeds I was attaining on downhills were more than 130 km/h. The bike computer could only go up to 130 km/h! We needed to build safety measures into the design wherever we could.

The ACT made provision that in the unconventional and HPV category you may either have a following vehicle or motorbike as support. In my case, I had an 11-seater bus following me, packed with enthusiastic supporters. They described the following incident to me, spectating it from the confines of the bus.

I was descending Hospital Bend at 100 km/h, about 5 km after the start. The road splits: to the right was the ACT route and the road going to the left was towards Cape Town International airport. I had a front-wheel blowout as I pulled the front brake. The person who put the front wheel in that morning, after transporting it to the event, did not check that the axle was set in deep enough into the slots of the fork. When I applied the brakes, they were not pulling and braking on the rim but the side of the tyre.

As I skidded and turned like a spinning top on the downhill at 100 km/h there was nothing I could do but wait for the impact against the curb of the island splitting the lanes. I was wondering, would I be going to the airport on the N2 or am I still on the route? Whilst spinning on my side the carbon fibre started burning and as it was still dark it created a spectacular display of fireworks. There was a real danger that the fairing could lose so much skin that I would be exposed to the road.

Luckily, I came to a standstill next to the curb. The team jumped out of the car expecting me to be fried inside, but the egg hatched. I was unscathed, got up and continued. A lot of credit can be given to the protection of space-age materials for mishaps like these.

GEROTEK WORLD RECORDS & CHAMPIONSHIPS

In 1992, the day before my world record attempt on the 12 and 24 hour distance records, I crashed in a test run. I lost skin on my arm when I dislodged from the fairing. The next day I had to ride heavily bandaged and broke the records.

Heavily bandaged I bettered the 24 hour record in 1992.

1993 Hour attempt on Gerotek, crashing at high speed after a front wheel blow-out. Our engineers were more interested in fixing the bike than the rider!

The next year, in the process of having a second attempt at the Hour record on the same day, I had a front-wheel tyre blowout. I crashed at more than 60 km/h. I lost skin on my arm and hip. I was bandaged and had a final go at the Hour.

At the 1993 World championships in Blaine, USA, the final event of the championships was the 1,000 m TT on the track. It was the last event for the evening, just as the mosquitoes were descending on Blaine. The Mississippi River had recently flooded most of the states it was flowing through and this caused a major mosquito problem. At that point in the heats, I had the second-fastest time. I had a final opportunity to go for gold and the title. I was ready and pumped.

With the 43-degree banking and typical racing speeds, one ought to be able to make a bike lean into the banking and stay perpendicular to the track, but not when you are doing over 80 km/h! To stay the course, you had to lean in more to the left, which meant you were close to horizontal to the ground. As I entered my second lap I was at top speed and as I leaned into the curve of the banking my fairing touched on the left of the inside of the track. This flipped and I skidded me up the banking and I hit the advertising barriers at the top, wheels first. Had they not been there I would have skidded, like a home run, out of the park! I came to a standstill in the middle of the back straight and the spectators expected the worst. However, I was unscathed and I hatched from the bike like a chicken from an egg. The crowd sighed a sigh of relief.

I was disappointed. The officials rushed over to find out if I was ok. My concern was the lost opportunity to go for gold. They then told me that I had 5 minutes allocated to complete my event and that I so far only used 2. I could restart. I rushed over to the start, got in and tried again. Gold medallist, Randy Lindley's time was nevertheless better than mine with a split second. He got gold and I silver. At least I supplied the adrenaline and the show!

THE MORE SERIOUS CRASHES
Not all mishaps occur in the setting of an organised event. I know of mountain bikers who play in rock gardens and in the process find new ways to collect the telephone numbers of nurses. Training can become as dangerous as races and sometimes more so because the needed medical assistance is not present. Luckily for me, in my most serious crash, medical assistance was there within seconds.

In 2014 I was completing my training and had to pass through a traffic intersection in Somerset West. It was downhill and normally my speed is around 60 km/h when I pass there on a green light. On this Sunday morning, as I entered the intersection, a lady driver turned in front of me and when she saw me, she froze. There was nothing I could do to avoid her. I hit her full on the passenger door side.

I had serious head and back injuries. Hysterically the woman jumped out of her car and tried to pull me up. In the process, she complicated my neck injuries. At that precise moment, there was a British lady doctor in the traffic, at the traffic light, who was being transported to the airport for her flight back home who came to my assistance and took charge so no one would move me until the paramedics arrived.

In Aug 2021 I was training through Stellenbosch before sunrise with fellow cyclist Jacques Jacobs. Whilst freewheeling downhill my bike suddenly swerved to the right and I landed face first into the tar. We suspect my top tube snapped and that made me lose control.

I lay unconscious next to the road for close to an hour with a broken back and arm at 3 C, causing me to become hypothermic. The irony was that I was lying less than 500 m away from the nearest hospital but there was no ambulance to transport me. An ambulance from a neighbouring town had to collect me.

They say there are two kinds of cyclists, those who have fallen and those who are about to fall. I suppose that would make me a red-blooded, pedigree cyclist. Though I was dubbed by the press, 'Ry & Val van der Merwe' I changed the name to 'Val & Ry van der Merwe'. I always got back on after the horse threw me off. I had a life to live!

11. THE GIFT – THE QUEEN OF COMEBACK

GOD PLACES SOME PEOPLE as a gift in your life. These are the ones that leave an indelible impression on your life, one of significance and influence. My late wife, Christa, was the most significant one in my life. I can honestly say that without her I would not have been the person I am today, would not have accomplished what I did and would not be fulfilling the purpose God has for my life.

As cyclists and men, we tease one another, by saying that they had to first get the boss' permission to do, train or go somewhere. This has never been said about Christa. I had an accommodating wife who excelled at simplicity, who was uncomplicated and my cheerleader.

I think it might be true about her what is rumoured about the wife of Winston Churchill. One day she and Winston were walking down Whitehall where they encountered Winston's wife's previous boyfriend before they were married. He was a manual labourer working at a building site. Winston remarked at her, 'just think about it. If you did not marry me, you would not have become the prime minister's wife.' Nonchalantly she replied, 'if you did not marry me, he would have been prime minister.'

Behind every successful man is a successful woman. I would even go so far as to say behind every successful cyclist is someone who feeds him, looks after his gear, tends to his wounds, passes him his water bottles, shouts the loudest next to the track, massages his legs and becomes his taxi when stuck with a breakdown next to the road. She was prepared to become a cycling widow but in turn, had the privilege of travelling the world when I competed overseas.

As a young couple, we toured South Africa with our luggage packed on the bike and rode together whilst studying in America.

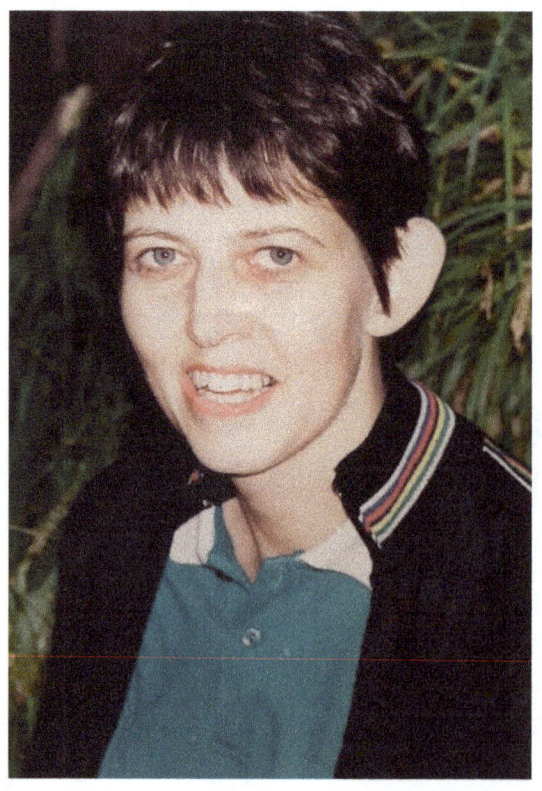

Christa van der Merwe

Christa had the privilege of accompanying me internationally on cycling excursions.

In 1980 we were nearly the winners of the Argus Cycle Tour. We rode tandem and broke away and gained a lead of just more than a minute when we punctured a kilometre from the finish in Camps Bay. The ACT was a fun ride then. You don't write off a good tubular and a rim for a fun ride. As we did not carry a spare tubular with us, we were stuck until one of our Matie teammates dropped off a tubular and we then completed the race. Had we known how important the Argus Cycle Tour would one day become we would have ridden the wheel to the hub to assure victory!

When doing personality and biometric tests for fun I was 'Hardy' and she was 'Softie'. I was the stone and she the cotton ball. If we both were the same there would have been sparks, but since we complemented each other perfectly I had the emotional space to be who I was and she, who she was meant to be.

She was diagnosed with terminal kidney failure in 2006 and due to failed knee operations became disabled. Due to her immobility, she had to sacrifice many things she could do before. Never did she complain or question God.

As I completed this book, fulfilling my promise to my wife, made five years before I started, she suddenly passed away. We did an amazing life together for 42 years. She had a tremendously positive influence on my life. She was royalty and simultaneously majored in simplicity. She

My tandem partner.

was an uncomplicated person, making life easy for everyone she encountered, allowing me the space to make life complicated whenever I felt compelled to.

Our relationship was a love story and divinely inspired. I only came to that realisation after her passing when in the packing of her belongings, we discovered her diary that she started on 7 Feb 1976, her first entry, the day she met me! Her first entry was as a first-year student at RAU during a get-to-know event between female and male dormitories.

Sat 7 Feb: 'I made closer acquaintance with Wimpie at the watermelon feast at Amper Daar's dining room. He stands next to me during the singing and comes and chat with me at the meal. He smears me with watermelon until my ears were filled with it. We walk back in the rain.'

Sunday 8 Feb: 'I see him at church. It happens so that he sits next to me at church. My heart pounds fiercely. He sits next to me at the movie afterwards. It amuses me how he digs up the courage to take my hand and tenderness towards him grows. I feel it is destined by God that we met each other and I leave it in His hands and allow him to take my hand.'

How perfect and what a Godly timing! This is God inspiring her to start chronicling her life the day she met her future husband. In the reading of the diary, I was reminded of the character traits of the woman I married, with who I did life together and got to know intimately. She loved unconditionally, forgave easily and drew the maximum she could out of every day.

Allowing me to discover this unknown diary of 45 years God works His miraculous ways. It eases the pain of loss and assures me that God was present and guiding right from the very first encounter. He was our guiding force in the good and bad times, in the 'for richer and for poorer' times and in the part 'until death us do part'.

I married the most awesome wife any man could imagine. Every skewed pot needs a perfectly fitted skewed lid. She complemented my skewness and together we formed the perfect pot. You only find this out years after saying 'I do'. She lived with my quirks and compensated for them. She compensated for my blind spots. She protected me spiritually. Her prayers encircled her family, but especially me. I could count on her protection.

I loved her dearly with all my heart and said to her at least once a day, 'I love you' and I meant it. A covenant of love bound us. We entrusted our hearts to one another. We felt safe in our vulnerability. We willingly stayed faithful to one another, being each other's soulmates. I thank God for the grace, when her health was failing, to handle it. In my own power, it was impossible.

At times, when she was bleeding internally, she would have uncontrollable diarrhoea of digested blood from her intestines. This could not be predicted and her clothes and bedding had to be changed regularly. I could not allow that events like these distract our focus from God and focus and shift it to a medical condition. That would have caused battle fatigue in her that would not easily be reversed.

When she attracted the dreaded Staphylococci bug in hospital, she was placed on the strongest antibiotic drip available for three months, but the bug did not want to die. It found a hiding place in her knees where the antibiotics could not reach. She dropped from 60 to 45 kg in this time. I received a call from her specialist one morning to inform me that they intended to physically remove bone and cartilage from her knees to rid her of the bacteria growing there. Even if the operation was performed, she would be too weak to survive, but they had no alternative. They advised us to come and say goodbye. They were planning the operation as the last one for the evening. They ought to be done by 20:00. After that, the theatre had to be disinfected.

We immediately activated a countrywide prayer response for her, informed the family and went to visit her, possibly for the last time. My best friend was lying in ICU, as always, smiling and encouraging those that visited her.

I phoned ICU at 20:00 to find out the progress. I was informed that they had one very unhappy patient with them, my wife. I was surprised and asked why? Did they do the operation? They replied that it was not needed as the bacteria died since speaking to me earlier that morning. God did a miracle on her behalf. I asked the sister why then is my wife unhappy? She replied, 'she is tired of hospital food and wants pizza'! Within half an hour I had a pizza on Christa's lap in ICU, as demanded.

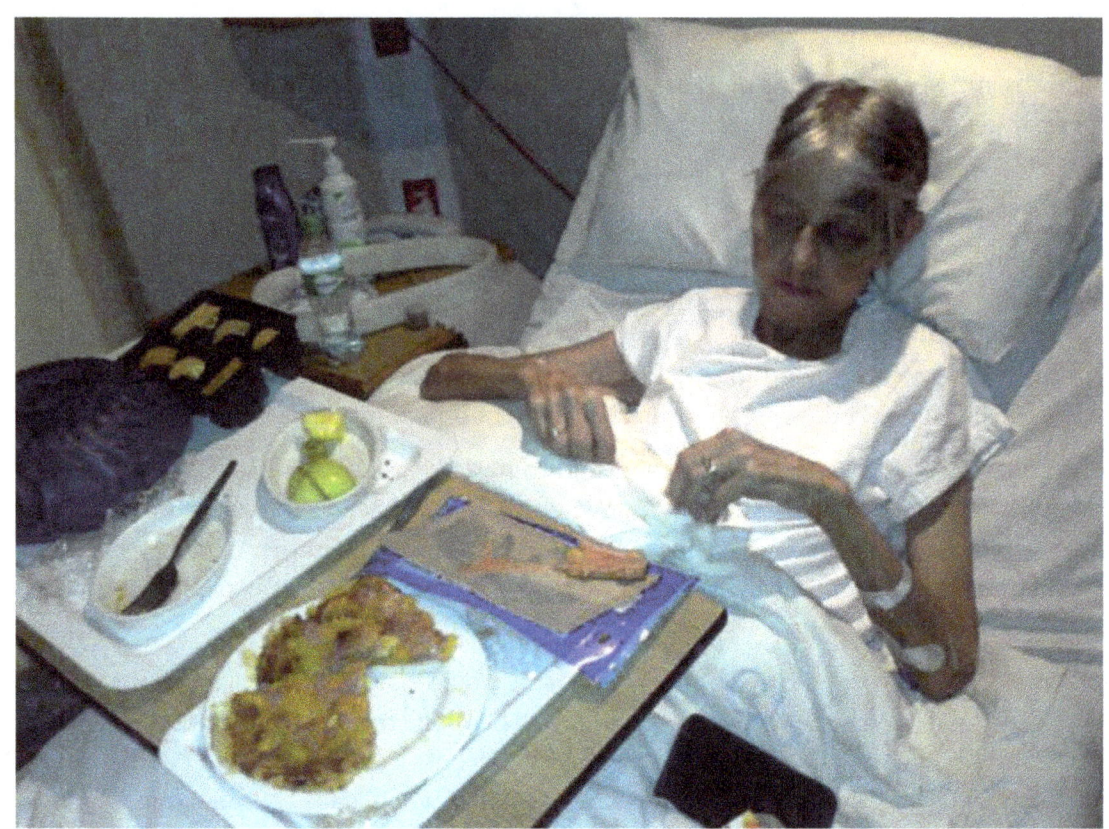

My wife's wish is my command, pizza it shall be!

As patients with kidney failure normally have a life expectancy of about five years God gave us fifteen sweet years, years filled with battles and sacrifice. As my wife started to become shorter, more brittle through osteoporosis and with foreseeable death approaching, she was growing in spiritual maturity. She was flexing her spiritual muscles through trials and suffering. Her condition lasted fifteen years of which she was in hospital for at least six and a half years. Never did she complain or express a regret that she was a victim of some sort. Never did she question God and ask Him, 'Why me?' She would have the attitude of 'Why not me?'

Through her trials and the way, she bore it, she reflected Christ in her and this testimony reached more people than her being without it. As a family, we knew death could happen at any moment and therefore we lived life with her to the fullest every day. She so wanted to be able to be part of my cycling activities, to travel the world, see André Rieu in Maastricht, but it was not possible, due to her being wheelchair-bound and always had to be close to a medical facility.

Her medical condition was one of increasing suffering. I perceived that her spiritual influence was increasing correspondingly. The enemy was sensing that she was populating heaven and denying him souls. She countered his marketing strategy with love and her smile. She had pain consistently for years. Due to her medical condition, she had to be careful of what she took as pain stillers.

Two months before she was promoted to glory, she complained of pain in her groin. Understanding that she was osteoporotic I advised her that she treat it as if she has a broken hip. We had it X-rayed, but this showed up negative. We were stuck with the lack of a diagnosis.

Her whole body was painful. The radiologist identified decreasing chest volume due to a shrinking of the rib cage. There was hardly space for her to breathe and for her heart to beat. It was impossible for her to lie in a prone position. The same day Christa and I had an appointment to see her specialist for the way forward I crashed heavily in the dark on my training ride which left me unconscious next to the roadside with a broken back and arm. Since I was the person lifting her in and out of the wheelchair, helping her to dress, bathe, etc. I could not do it anymore due to my condition.

God provided us with angels, sometimes people we didn't know, who appear at our door, early morning, to come and help Christa wash and dress, things only another woman can do. We realised this could not go on indefinitely as Christa lost all independence. She needed medical help and could only return once she regained some form of independence. As we discussed our options, she looked me in the eyes and said, 'I will not be coming back home'. I thought she meant she will not be returning home but to something like a frail care facility, as a sub-acute hospital. It was as if she had a premonition of what was to come.

She was admitted to hospital and an MRI was done and this indicated a hip fracture, something they could not pick up on X-rays. What became apparent as one of the causes for her continuous pain was the number of broken ribs. We were not aware that ribs were broken. They were treated as soft tissue injuries whilst they were actually fractures. She became my glass doll. The orthopaedic surgeon advised that he would be doing a hip replacement on her. It was risky as she had brittle bones but he would use a special calcium cement to glue the prosthesis to her femur and not use plates and screws.

I emphasised to the doctors that due to previous encounters with general anaesthetics and pain killers she nearly lost her life. Had it not been that I was sitting next to her whilst she was sleeping, after being released from the hospital, after the removal of her wisdom teeth and hearing that she stopped breathing, she would have died years ago. With this as background, I asked them to take special care with the opiates.

An hour before the operation was due, I received a call from the anaesthetist to warn me that they have just done an echogram on her and that the chances of her surviving the operation were minimal. The calcium cement posed no threat to a normal patient but in her case, since her chemical balances as a dialysis patient was so critical, that if anything came into her bloodstream and something went wrong, they had no recourse. They could revive her only either by breathing for her or just beating her heart for her but could not do both at the same time. The chest cavity did not allow that. They advised against the procedure.

To them, the options were death or a broken hip and lying in bed with it for the rest of her life with the accompanying pain.

I advised them that we should ask Christa herself. Christa refused further pain and said there was a third option: operation and faith that God would do a miracle and help her survive. Due to her choice and the severity of the operation they decided to postpone the operation for two days and give the family time to come and say goodbye.

By now Christa became known as the Queen of Comeback, having survived so many previous encounters and brushes with death before. If she did not receive dialysis she would die. They saved her life three times a week for the past fifteen years. We did not fear death anymore, but suffering and not being able to help the person suffering intimidated me.

The operation was a success. She survived the procedure. The surgeon predicted that her pain would cease nearly immediately, which was the case for Christa. After a day she was complaining of the same pain. Due to handling by the staff, the leg broke next to the joint of the prosthesis. They could not do another hip replacement.

The surgeon phoned me in Johannesburg, as I was there for a short business trip, to inform me of her condition and said that her suffering is inhumane. They were planning a leg transplant as the last option, but a further complication arose. She was bleeding internally. They could not wait. They had a donor. Her whole femur would be removed and the prosthesis joined in the new bone. At the same time, they would search for the leak with a camera.

I raced back from Johannesburg whilst the operation was in progress and arrived at the ICU as she was coming out of the recovery room. She was weak but happy. She survived the operation. She now became the Queen of Comeback and Fightback. However, the internal bleeding was taking its toll.

An hour into her last dialysis her blood pressure fell to something in the forties over thirty-one. She was in a critical state. Her friend, Sanet van der Merwe, recalls that she gave the technician instruction to end the

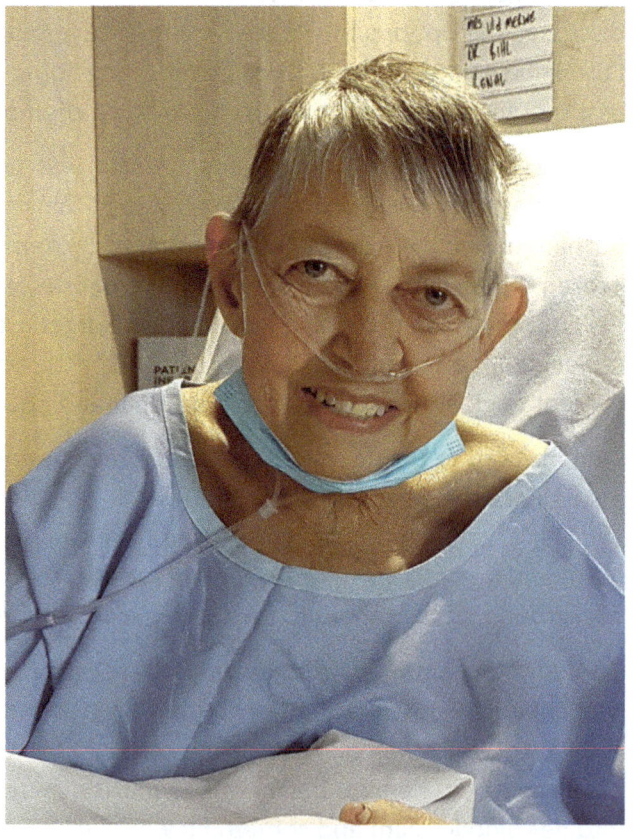

Christa spent 6.5 years in total in hospitals in her last 15 years, always smiling.

session and to remove the pipes. My fighter had crossed the line. The race was over. It was time to take her place in the pavilion of faith heroes to encourage us who were still in the race.

She refused further treatment, as well as food and water. They placed her in the 'death room' so family and friends could visit her privately and uninterrupted. My son, Chris, and I were the last to see her, to say goodbye. These were disturbingly holy moments. I have never accompanied anyone before to the gates of Heaven. The face of death is ugly and these images would possibly stay with me forever. However, the privilege of being present at the last moments of someone passing over to eternity has a lasting effect.

The image I have of Christa in life is one of a warhorse. They don't flinch in battle. They obey the rider's command fully. They are not distracted by the sounds of battle. They would even run directly into the spears of the opposing force if called for it. She did not flinch at the battles ahead. She experienced battle three times a week for fifteen years without ceasing. At times she turned at death's door, laughed in its face and still maintained her faith and kept the course. She had all the excuses to quit at her disposal. No one would have resented her for choosing the easy way out or to complain. Instead, she still chose to lead by serving others.

Together we lost an unborn child and together we bore the loss bravely and with God's grace. She is reunited with our unknown daughter in heaven. She consistently blessed others with little miracles, smiles and encouragement. She healed those with broken wings with love and patience.

As a soldier and sportsman, I recognize courage. I appreciate perseverance. I value determination and tenacity. These concepts are a necessity and to become an expert I need to practise them to excel in sport. My soulmate was my superior and I could learn from her.

God did not give her a miracle. He gave her His grace to overcome what life hurled at her. Every time she was bowled a curveball, she hit it out of the park. She did not allow the enemy to defeat her. She did not lose a race or a fight, but actually completed it and decided to end it once she crossed the line victoriously!

I realise I am not the hero but I received a hero for a wife, a precious gift from God, the Queen of Comeback, whom I had the privilege to do life with for 42 years.

12. FINGERPRINTS

WHEN A CRIME was committed, investigators search for fingerprints to identify the responsible parties or those who were involved or were on the scene. Fingerprints are unique and leave the trail where you have been. By touching anything you leave not only your fingerprints behind but traces of your DNA. This identifies you. Your fingerprint is the hallmark and cornerstone of your identity.

Many people and incidents have touched my life, some more than others. I can identify their fingerprints on my life as I leave an imprint on the lives of others, intentionally or unintentional, for good or for bad. I can identify some people as influencers in my life and incidents that had a lasting effect. Through their example, either good or bad, I learnt how I do and do not want to be like and whether I want to follow in their footsteps. I might have an equal dose of bad experiences of individuals who nudged me in a direction, causing a reaction to being the opposite of their example.

We all leave fingerprints on the lives of others. Interaction with people has lasting effects. As a person of influence, I realize the responsibility that goes along with it. I never aspired to be anyone's role model, but cannot help that someone does follow what I do or don't, what I say or don't.

I have never really had heroes or mentors who I would have liked to follow, people who purposefully set themselves at task to mould me and me following their mentorship willingly. Yes, there were and are people that I admire, possibly for different reasons than what one would expect. I admire a person who, like an underdog, overcomes or beats the favourite. The favourite might be the hero and the underdog unknown. I do not necessarily aspire to be like or imitate either of them, though I admire them.

I have a particular, unique reason for being, for existing. I live an authentic life, not someone else's. I do not copy someone's life or live life by proxy. As unique as my fingerprints are, so unique am I and God's purpose for me. I am that one unique piece in the puzzle. I write my unique history. For something to become history, it had to become lived future first. Therefore, the influence someone or something had on my life becomes valid when I measure it and it enforces my WHY. It should help me to make it possible for me to live my WHY.

> *'I continuously strive to be the best I can be and live an abundant life, a life of contentment, a life of no regrets. I challenge man-made and perceived limits. I challenge the status quo and write my own history.'*

Yet, being a very independent person, I realise I would not have been the person I am today or would not have achieved most of what I did, had it not been for the nudging and contribution of certain individuals. Most of these nudgings were unintentional but had an effect that I could identify as course-changers. When a rocket is launched to a far-off planet it is small adjustments early on that save major adjustments and fuel later on when the rocket is off course. The lack of small adjustments could mean missing the planet by millions of kilometres.

Early and gentle bending and forming, when the tree is still a twig, save it later on from the danger of breaking when it is a full-grown tree and the same action takes place. This is especially true for the impressionable and the young. People who helped me reach a destination are valued because God allowed them to be His instrument to make a small adjustment early on. God even used the evil intentions of individuals as nudging to alter my course, to accelerate or to decrease the trip towards the destination.

I believe the processes involved afterwards are as significant as the event of the nudging. Some may think reaching the destination is the climax, but sometimes, more importantly, is the journey, the processes of working with the good and bad experiences. Having a baked and decorated cake cannot occur without the process of baking. Baking cannot occur without having the ingredients. The ingredients will be useless without a recipe. All of these are equally important. Salt on its own is repulsive, as is food without it. The end product of who you are is in the combination of the good and the bad that occurred in life. By embracing the effect of both assures me that I can live a life of abundance and go to the grave without regrets.

Having had both abundance and lack, Paul says, he lives a life of contentment. Having had a life of the fingerprints of people on my life both with evil and Godly intents, I strive to live a life of gratefulness.

CHALLENGING THE LIMITS
Challenging physical boundaries was possibly due to us having massive trees in our garden. They became the objects of personal challenges by climbing to the uttermost top. I can remember as a three-year-old it was not always just to get to the top, but to get there in the fastest time, up and down. This created a strong 'I can' and confidence. These were the seeds for challenging the status quo. To me trees were made to climb, why else would God place them on the earth? For the same reason, why do records exist? To be broken.

I could remember that from this one particular tree you could see the whole neighbourhood. My mother travelled by bus from work. I could normally see her arriving and walking home, coming along the sidewalk. Many afternoons I would wait for her arrival by sitting right at the top of the tree and greeting her. My mother was terrified that I would tumble out of the tree. I, on the other hand then wanted to show her how fast I could come down to meet her. This climbing of trees nudged me to develop a daring and fearless attitude early on.

BUILDING MEMORIES

There are three 'hot buttons' in life. They are 'do', 'be' and 'buy'. What do you want to do? What do you want to be? What do you want to buy? They are the basic activators to trigger people into motion.

During school holidays many of my schoolmates had the opportunity to do casual work and earn an income with which they bought something they wanted. I can remember that I made a wilful and quality decision that I shall create memories during the holidays. I was activated by what I wanted to do. I had the wisdom to know that whatever earnings bought would eventually be forgotten, but the memories I collected I will always have and I would be able to one day share with my grandchildren.

Deciding what I wanted to do in my life and what I wanted to be helped me to become the author of my life. I take responsibility for my decisions. By living with my decisions, I have no one to blame and in effect no regrets. I could live a life of contentment.

THE BULLIES

I had my fair share of bullies in life and still do. These are the people who abuse their position to impose, who abuse authority, or who, due to poor self-image ridicule you verbally or belittle you in the presence of others. I had the bullies who became physical, but somehow, I sorted them out early through the confidence I acquired through Judo. I did not need to fight them, because I knew I could give them a good thrashing. My confidence, amid their threats, refrained them from continuing.

As a child at school, my friends were academically outstanding and the Jocks, who were not academically sound, made them out as the nerds. I was their 'protector', but due to my association with them were demeaned, by being called a 'trassie' (homosexual). It is in my DNA to protect the weak and support the underdog. These actions and incidences had the lasting effect of creating a resolute 'I will'. It was like trying to push me off a cliff. The harder you push, the more and harder I resist.

CYCLISTS AS BULLIES

In cycling, there were the rough and "dirty" riders of my time, especially on the track. They were like a gang, at times becoming physical on the bike, whether head butting, elbow and shoulder shoving. This made me fast because no one could do this to me whilst in front. Their verbal demeaning was their way to intimidate, on and off the bike. It was possible that they knew I could or would not retaliate as a Christian and they abused this as a privilege to make me a verbal punching bag.

I do know how the abuse ended when I stooped down to their level. It was an evening race on the Bellville track. In this particular race, as we were coming for the sprint we were on the banking, entering the home straight, Wiele Wentzel was on my inside below me. With his right hand, he reached forward, grabbed me on the hip and was about to fling himself forward and myself backwards when something in me flipped. I whacked him with my left hand with a backhand that a tennis pro would be proud of. That was the last this ever happened. The word must have spread under the abusers and from that day onwards the abuse never occurred again.

Being a good amateur, it was inevitable that by competing against the pros for the same prize money it was perceived that you were taking food out of their mouths, though amateurs had financial commitments too. I was a threat and treated as such. Whenever we competed in the same race their domestiques were tasked to counter any move I make to ensure that the outcome will not be in favour of an amateur. This explains why, I believe, I could achieve more in the international arena, outside of SA. There was no one to mark me. I could perform at my potential.

For some, this animosity continued off the bike too. Many of them lacked the professionalism that I experienced in Europe where you battle fiercely on the bike and afterwards have the greatest of times together.

It was in the 1982 Rapport Tour, as we were entering Pretoria for the stage finish, that one of Alan van Heerden's High Way Electrical members, Jannie van der Berg, attacked and I chased him down. Alan van Heerden was known for his ill-temper. As the bunch eased up he angrily swore at me and humiliated me in the bunch, as if I have had an obligation to his team, lecturing me that I should not have chased down a fellow South African.

It was rather humiliating and an embarrassing moment for the others, like a parent scolding his child in public and you don't know where to look and what to say. Something in me had had enough. A red line was crossed. I slapped him with a flat hand on the back. If he had false teeth or a glass eye, they would have ended up on the road. The whole bunch cheered, except his team, of course, because someone had the guts to stand up for this abusive behaviour.

That was the last he or any pro ever again abused the privilege of my restraint to use me as a verbal punching bag. Until Van Heerden's death, we had a good relationship and mutual respect. He was the one pro I could speak to directly and call a spade a spade. As a fellow team member of the 1977 Solly Kramers team, he used to throw his toys out of the cot and made a spectacle if he did not get what he wanted. I warned him that being well known does not give anyone a licence to be ill-mannered.

THE SOUTH AFRICAN CYCLING FEDERATION (SACF) AS BULLIES

Bullies made their appearances in different forms. When people of no consequence are given some power, they always tend to abuse it. I have always had a good feel for fairness. If something isn't fair it draws my attention like a magnet. Like a business transaction, for it to be fair the purchased article and the value one parts with should balance out. If not, it is not a fair trade. This same sense of fairness lacked with Federation officials when applying rules. It was the 'small' men who wanted to make the biggest noise and project influence and power. They were the ones being unjust in their applying of rules and governing the sport.

I was suspended from Western Province cycling several times. Once was for 3 weeks because I did not appear at a track meet, though I never entered. The media normally create showdowns between competitors before meetings. This sells tickets in the stands and newspapers. In this particular instance, they created a showdown between me and Leon Jonker. However, I had other commitments that weekend and did not enter. This embarrassed Western Province Cycling and the club organising the event because there was no showdown. Instead of reprimanding the newspaper reporter for creating fake news, the cyclist gets a suspension.

In another incident, I was suspended for 2 weeks because I did not arrive at a SA track championship in Welkom to compete for the Western province team in only one event, the team pursuit. As a student, it was expected of me to pay for myself to get there from Cape Town to participate for a provincial team instead of the province covering the expenses fully of whoever they selected. I informed the team manager in advance of my absence due to the lack of funds. I was assured that they do have a reserve they could use if I cannot make it. Irrespective of that I was still suspended for 2 weeks.

It was forbidden to compete in the Argus Cycle Tour as a licensed rider. Hugh Dale, chairman of Western Province Cycling would go to the finish and search for registered riders that he saw in the crowd or crossing the line. Jonathan Heard and myself were once suspended for being seen at the ACT, though we have not entered or participated, but seen on the course. It was deemed that our presence gave legitimacy to the Pedal Power Association. Our constitutional right to be where we wanted to be was restricted at will by power-hungry individuals.

The SACF took my licence away in middle 1987 because, according to their rules, I should have declared a sponsorship in Namibia where I would compete as the cyclist in a team triathlon in Dec 1987. Take note, this was in a different country and for a different sports discipline: triathlon. They wrongly claimed that they could lay claim to part of my sponsorship as the individual sponsorship rules of the time made provision for. That rule only made provision for if you were to apply the sponsorship in their events and wanted to create exposure for your sponsor in any of their events, which would not have occurred because it was not in a cycling event and neither in their jurisdiction.

In the meanwhile, I competed with a Belgian licence in the world championships in Europe. On the return, when the issue could not be resolved by normal means and the date of the SA championships approached where I had to defend my SA title, I took it to the High Court in Cape Town and requested through an urgent appeal to set the suspension aside so I could defend my SA title the next day. The High Court rejected the request of my legal team. As explained to me later, the basis was that it should not be a matter that should be heard in a court. The Federation should be able to handle this in fairness. It was so obvious to the court that the decision was unfair and they felt that a sports body should be able to see the merits of my case and decide in my favour.

However, the SACF did not see the obvious merits and suspended me for life on the Friday. The SA Road champs were the next day. There was no way I could appeal the decision in court in time as the championship was then already a completed fact. I just left the case as it was and handed them and the case over to God.

There are several occasions in my career where certain senior officials, who had their daggers ready for me, abused their positions in either the SACF or when acting as an official at races. I truly do believe that the abuse and unfairness did not escape the attention of God either. He avenged me and rewarded me greatly in return, giving me much more than what I could think or ask for, what I was deprived of, whether it was titles or opportunities. I was richly blessed in both. God is not blind and restored to me that which was stolen and what I was deprived of.

The bullies from different camps sometimes team up together. The saying, my enemy's enemy is my friend, has truth, looking back at the 1985 Rapport Tour when both professional cyclists and the SACF, who clashed regularly, allied to expel me from the Tour and give me a 3-month suspension. Very few know the true background for this and this could set the record straight.

A day before the 1985 Tour started a couple of us sat in the lounge of the hotel where we were staying. Lappe Laubscher, a reporter of Rapport, came to sit with us and asked us a couple of questions. One was whether we think South African riders are using drugs to enhance their performance? Robbie McIntosh was just suspended from the Tour of Portugal and fined and would be competing as a favourite in the Rapport Tour. Willie Engelbrecht, one of the riders present, confirmed that he knows they do use and he knows who. I confirmed that I know of an overseas rider who rode the Rapport Tour before, who supplied some of our revered cyclists with the needed anabolic steroids, whilst competing in Europe. The conversation continued, the normal pre-tour chit-chat of who could be favourites, etc. At that time, I had just completed my masters on the question about the abuse of drugs in sports.

The Sunday, a couple of days later, during the Tour, it was front page and headline, 'South African riders 'byte on' stimulants – Chaplain (a fellow cyclist) reveals' and my name used as the source. This led to a revolt by the professional riders, some who ironically had been caught positive in the past, who demanded my head and that of Lappe Laubscher who wrote the article. If not, they would withdraw from the Tour.

I was heard by the SACF in Beaufort West, fined and warned. My constitutional right to speak to whom I wanted to was curbed by them too. They ordered that I may not speak to the press. As I left the meeting, some of the press was waiting outside the room. I mentioned that I stick to what I have said (what I said to Lappe Laubscher). However, the SACF was still under the impression that I have named professionals by name or by implication. Engelbrecht was more specific, but I reckon because I have studied the subject of the abuse of drugs in sport, I was a more credible source to Lappe.

The following morning as we were about to depart on the stage from Beaufort West to Oudtshoorn, all hell broke loose. I was suspended from the tour and suspended for 3 months from all cycling. I went to Lappe Laubscher and demanded that he reveal exactly who said

Boikot afgeweer ná bewerings oor doepa
Wimpie geskors uit fietstoer

Van COLIN HOFFMANN

OUDTSHOORN. — Wimpie van der Merwe, kaptein van Padveiligheid se Weermag-fietsryspan in vanjaar se Rapport-Toer, is gister hier geskors en mag nie verder deelneem nie. Hy is op die koop toe ook vir ses weke uit alle fietsry geskors.

Dié optrede teen Van der Merwe spruit regstreeks uit 'n berig in die Sondagkoerant Rapport waarin hy beweer het dat hy weet van fietsryers in Suid-Afrika wat opkikkers gebruik. Hy is vroeër ook met R50 beboet omdat hy strydig met die reëls van die Suid-Afrikaanse Fietsryfederasie verklarings aan die pers gedoen het.

Van der Merwe se skorsing het 'n dreigende boikot deur vyf van die voorste beroepspanne afgeweer, hoewel die beroepsfietsryers nog nie hul sin gekry het met hul eis dat die verslaggewer wat die berig geskryf het, ook teruggestuur word nie. Van der Merwe keer vandag na Pretoria terug.

Die straf teen hom is gistermiddag laat op 'n perskonferensie deur die bestuur van die Suid-Afrikaanse Fietsryfederasie bekend gemaak. Dit het gevolg op 'n amptelike klag deur mnr. Arthur Rice, voorsitter van die Beroepsfietsry-unie, nadat Van der Merwe sedert ...

toekoms in fietsry te gesels. "Ons kan dit moontlik oorweeg om te eis dat amateur-jaers nie meer aan padwedrenne deelneem nie."

Van Heerden het gesê die amateurs beskuldig die beroepsjaers daarvan dat hulle opkikkers gebruik "omdat ons beter as hulle is. Het een van hulle al daaraan gedink om die wêreld te vertel hoe hard ons werk vir wat ons graag wil bereik?"

Van die ander jaers het reguit gesê hulle sal nooit weer aan 'n Rapport-Toer deelneem nie. Een van hulle Theuns Mulder van VFP-Produkte se span, het ...

Beneke hangs on to Tour lead

OUDTSHOORN. — Tony Impey, a skilled time triallist, caught a lively bunch off-guard in the Rapport cycling tour to win the 187-km sixth stage from Beaufort-West to Oudtshoorn yesterday.

Mark Beneke is still holding on determinedly to his yellow jersey as the overall leader. He finished the stage claiming bunch time and starts today's stage nine seconds ahead of his younger brother Gary ...

go for a win. He has the fastest time for the 20 kilometre individual time trial and he put that talent to good use after the sting had been taken out of the sprinters in the bunch ...

The TV-4 squad unseated Alan van Heerden's Southern Sun-Peugeot squad and will set off on the 112 kilometre stage to Mossel Bay today with a three second lead ...

what as I was being punished for something I am not guilty of. He went to a commissioner of oaths to confirm under oath what I have said, which was contrary to what I have been punished for. None of the officials of either the Rapport Tour or SACF wanted to entertain that piece of evidence because they were threatened by the professionals to withdraw from the Tour. The action was led by Mark Beneke, according to news reports.

I had an interesting conversation with the Tour director, Raoul de Villiers, as he was taking me to the airport and I realised how rigged the system was. He admitted that SA cyclists used prohibited substances and that there is abuse on the Rapport Tour, in the past and possibly in that specific edition of the Tour.

That same day several riders were caught positive. They got time and monetary penalties and could continue the Tour whilst a whistleblower on the subject was suspended. He said, even if it is true that SA cyclists use the prohibited substances, we cannot talk about it. It would endanger the future of the Tour as they would lose sponsors. I was the fall guy, the scapegoat to save the Rapport Tour.

As in the Lance Armstrong case. For years there were denials, until one day someone dared to break the omerta. The whistleblowers, from the press up to a fellow cyclist, were vilified and even taken to and threatened with court action. Years later the same started happening in SA. Retired riders from teams where they were using substances, started talking. There were no more holds on them.

As one said to me, he was told in so many words, if he doesn't use and doesn't perform, he will lose his contract. It was blackmail. Once you used it you always had to deny the use of it or the fact that you participated will be revealed. It makes me think the overreaction of the professionals from the time, was an admission of guilt if you compare the similarity of denials and counter-accusations of the Armstrong saga playing off in the decade of his reign as Tour de France winner. The abuse in SA was possibly even among the amateurs. There was however no reaction from top amateurs on the Rapport Tour, claiming that they were falsely accused.

I was lying in hospital for two days a couple of years back. Across from me was another patient who was one of the top polygraphists in SA. He uses lie detector tests in his investigations and had just cracked a very prominent murder case with his polygraph test. I asked him if the test can be manipulated and he said that if the questions are asked correctly, there is zero chance to lie without being detected.

I told him about my experience with top cyclists who deny that they have ever used prohibited substances in their cycling career. In the end, it will be my word against their word. He made a suggestion. If I am ever challenged about the truthfulness of my statements by anyone who I know or suspected to have been one of these riders, he would be willing to do polygraphs for me on anyone who denies the facts. This will expose the truth or the lie.

When I arrived at my base in Pretoria from the Rapport Tour my commanding officer received a call from a dizzy height, from general Witkop Badenhorst. He was fuming fire and brimstone

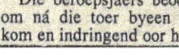

Twee gestraf, een bly weg vir opkikkertoets
Drie Portugese vas oor doepa

Van COLIN HOFFMANN

CERES. — Twee Portugese fietsryers in vanjaar se Rapport-Toer, Marco Chagas en Paolo Ferreira, is daaraan skuldig bevind dat hulle opkikkers gebruik het en gister swaar gestraf. Die uitslae van die toetse wat eergister op hulle uitgevoer is, was positief.

Nog een van hul landgenote, Manuel Cunha, het nie opgedaag vir 'n opkikkertoets wat gistermiddag ná die agtste skof tussen Worcester en Ceres gelas is nie. Die skeidsregters het beslis dat dieselfde straf aan hom opgelê sal word as aan Chagas en Ferreira.

Die drie is onmiddellik ingevolge die internasionale reëls met 1 000 Switserse frank elk beboet. Chagas en Ferreira verbeur ook alle pryse en tydbonusse wat hulle in die skof tussen Oudtshoorn en Mosselbaai gewen het en Cunha alles wat hy gister verdien het. Hy was derde in die skof.

Al drie word na die laaste plek in die uitslag van die 30ste plek. Cunha se nuwe posisie sal eers vandag bepaal word omdat party van die skeidsregters gisteraand op Worcester oornag het en die ander op Ceres. Hulle kon gevolglik nie byeenkom nie.

Mnr. Alves het gedreig dat hy ná die toer 'n verklaring sal doen wat die Suid-Afrikaanse fietsrywêreld sal skud. Hy wou nie daaroor uitwei nie,

Nog sport op bl. 24, 26, 27 en 28

---

about the fact that I was suspended and the Defence Force will not allow anyone to use drugs in sport and that my drug use will be followed up with further disciplinary actions. My CO had to halt him right there and explain to him that the heading that he saw in that morning's newspaper, 'Wimpie suspended from cycle tour' was not due to the fact of use, but being part of exposing it.

For weeks I had to clarify this misunderstanding to supporters, family and friends. Some read of the suspension or heard it, misunderstood it, could not clarify it and eventually just lived with it, always with the impression I was suspended because of the use of drugs.

These are the fingerprints fellow cyclists left, who used illegal, physically enhancing substances, not only on my life but the rest of the cycling community's. As in the prominent case of Armstrong, it was a life of lies. The press built rag dolls, false egos and hot air personas around the performances of some of these riders who were performing above their potential. Sponsors were selling their products and linking their image to these false personas, suspecting or did not care whether their riders were on something.

Some young children fell in love with the images of the cyclists the press helped create as household names. These young children are not young anymore and as adults still revere

Portugese oor opkikkers vas in fietstoer

VAN COLIN HOFFMANN

CERES. — Twee Portugese fietsryers in vanjaar se Rapport-Toer, Marco Chagas en Paolo Ferreira, is daaraan skuldig bevind dat hulle opkikkers gebruik het en gister swaar gestraf. Die uitslae van die toetse wat eergister op hulle uitgevoer is, was positief.

Nog een van hul landgenote, Manuel Cunha, het nie opgedaag vir 'n opkikkertoets wat gistermiddag ná die agtste skof tussen Worcester en Ceres gelas is nie. Die skeidsregters het beslis dat dieselfde straf aan hom opgelê sal word as aan Chagas en Ferreira.

Die drie is onmiddellik ingevolge die internasionale reëls met 1 000 Switserse frank elk beboet. Chagas en Ferreira verbeur ook alle pryse en tydbonusse wat hulle in die skof tussen Oudtshoorn en Mosselbaai gewen het en Cunha alles wat hy gister verdien het. Hy was derde in die skof.

Al drie word na die laaste plek in die uitslag van die betrokke skofte afgeskuif en daar word 10 minute by hul algehele tyd bygelas. Boonop word hulle geskors vir een maand, opgeskort vir een jaar, het brig. Arno Combrink, toesighouer by die neem van die monsters, gisteraand bekend gemaak.

"Hulle word as eerste oortreders beskou," het hy gesê. Die verbode bestanddeel amfetamien is in die monsters gevind wat by Chagas en Perreira geneem en in die laboratorium by die Vrystaatse Universiteit in Bloemfontein ontleed is.

Hoewel Chagas, 'n vorige wenner van die Rapport-Toer, en Ferreira, wat tot voor gister nog in die algehele tweede plek was, verder mag deelneem, het die onderbestuurder van die Portugese Sunripe Fruits-span, mnr. Orlando Alves, skerp gereageer en eers gedreig om sy jaers aan die toer te onttrek. Hy het die Suid-Afrikaanse Fietsryfederasie van 'n wraak-aksie beskuldig.

"Dis die federasie se wraak omdat Robbie McIntosh vroeër vanjaar in Portugal skuldig bevind is," het hy gesê. Hy het verwys na die bevinding in die Toer van Portugal dat die Suid-Afrikaanse beroepsjaer ook amfetamien gebruik het.

Die Portugese se skuldigbevinding is 'n groot terugslag vir hul span. Ferreira word nou afgeskuif tot in die 25ste plek en Chagas van die 29ste tot die 30ste plek. Cunha se nuwe posisie sal eers vandag bepaal word omdat party van die skeidsregters gisteraand op Worcester oornag het en die ander op Ceres. Hulle kon gevolglik nie byeenkom nie.

Mnr. Alves het gedreig dat hy ná die toer 'n verklaring sal doen wat die Suid-Afrikaanse fietsrywêreld sal skud. Hy wou nie daaroor uitwei nie, maar het wel gesê in 1982 en 1983 is die toetse nie na behore uitgevoer nie.

Hy het beweer dat die toerdokter, dr. Koos Marais, gister aan hom beken het dat daar reeds in die eerste toets ná die eerste skof spore van 'n verbode bestanddeel in Ferreira se monster aangetref is. Dr. Marais het gesê dit was egter nie genoeg om 'n skuldigbevinding te regverdig nie.

"Hoekom vertel hy my dit eers vandag?" het mnr. Alves gesê. "Hoekom het

● Vervolg op bl. 24 ●

Nog sport op bl. 24, 26, 27 en 28

● Vervolg van bl. 30 ●

hy toe gesê die uitslag van die toets op Paolo was negatief? Daar is iets verdags."

Brig. Combrink het mnr. Alves se aantygings as onsin verwerp. "Ek het vooraf gewaarsku dat geen inligting, hoe sleg ook al, weerhou sou word nie. Almal het geweet dat ons vanjaar baie streng sou optree," het hy gesê.

"Hulle kan ook nie sê dat ons op hulle pik nie. Daar was meer as genoeg Suid-Afrikaners betrokke by die drie reekse toetse wat ons tot dusver uitgevoer het. Buitendien weet die mense in die laboratorium nie watter jaers se monsters hulle ontleed nie. Elke monster word net genommer," het brig. Combrink gesê.

Mnr. Raoul de Villiers, voorsitter van die Suid-Afrikaanse Fietsryfederasie, het gesê dit is jammer dat dit met die Portugese gebeur het, maar die Rapport-Toer word volgens die internasionale reëls aangebied. "Ons het almal vooraf gewaarsku en kom die internasionale reëls streng na.

"Dit is geen wraak-aksie teen die Portugese nie. Hulle het hulle die probleme self op die hals gehaal," het mnr. De Villiers gesê.

McIntosh, op wie gisteraand weer 'n toets uitgevoer is, wou niks sê nie, behalwe dat daar "nou weer baie beskuldiginge rondgeslinger sal word. Ek hou my daaruit, want ek wil nie betrokke raak nie."

Mnr. Francisco Nunes, voorsitter van die Portugese Fietsryfederasie wat mnr. De Villiers se persoonlike gas op die toer is, was een van die eerste mense wat van die uitslag verwittig is. "Hy het die uitslag aanvaar en niks verder te sê gehad nie," het brig. Combrink gesê.

Cunha, McIntosh en Alan van Heerden, wenner van gister se skof, is ná die skof op Ceres in kennis gestel dat daar toetse op hulle uitgevoer sou word. Die twee Suid-Afrikaners het hulle betyds aangemeld, maar Cunha het weggebly.

Ingevolge die reëls is hom 'n halfuur gegun om hom aan te meld. Dr. Marais en brig. Combrink het 'n uur gewag en, toe hy nie opdaag nie, het hulle besluit dat sy afwesigheid 'n skuldbekentenis is.

Gister se uitslae

CERES. — Die uitslae van en die posisies ná gister se agtste skof in die Rapport-Toer is:

Agtste skof (Worcester na Ceres, 137,9 km): 1. Alan van Heerden (Peugeot/Southern Sun) 3:44:58; 2. Robbie McIntosh (SAUK–TV4) 3:44:59; 3. Manuel Cunha (Sunripe Fruits) 3:45:00; 4. Anthony Martini (Tlokwe), Mark Beneke (VFP-Produkte), Rodney Fowler (Peugeot-/Southern Sun) 3:45:01; 7. Ertjies Bezuidenhout (Peugeot/Southern Sun) 3:46:56; 8. Steven Wolhuter (Padveiligheid) 3:46:57; 9. Craig Nash (VPF-Produkte) 3:46:58; 10. Willie Engelbrecht (Tlokwe) 3:46:05.

Algeheel: 1. Mark Beneke 28:15:48; 2. Alan van Heerden 28:17:13; 3. Robbie McIntosh 28:17:48; 4. Gary Beneke (Peugeot/Southern Sun) 28:18:15; 5. Johnny Koen (SAUK–TV4) 28:18:18; 6. Manual Cunha 28:18:35; 7. Anthony Martini 28:18:39; 8. Rodney Fowler 28:18:41; 9. Livio Mora (Pickfords) 28:18:47; 10. Michael Thomson (Imperial Truck Hire) 28:20:13.

Spankompetisie: 1. Pickfords 84:51:37; 2. Peugeot/Southern Sun 84:53:50; 3. VFP-Produkte 84:56:57; 4. Sunripe Fruits 84:57:50; 5. Tlokwe 84:59:48; 6. SAUK–TV4 85:06:18; 7. Imperial Truck Hire 85:14:12; 8. Padveiligheid 85:33:29; 9. Wes-Wits 87:00:53.

SA Eagle se Bergkoning: 1. Alan van Heerden 30; 2. Manuel Cunha 25; 3. Franco Bellardi (Pickfords) 21; 4. Mishak Moshisha (Wes-Wits) 19; 5. Venceslau Fernandes (Sunripe Fruits) 14; 6. Gavin Mulvenna (Imperial Truck Hire) 13; 7. Mark Beneke, 8. Ertjies Bezuidenhout 12; 9. Alfons Radipudi (Wes-Wits) 11; 10. Fourie Kotzé (Imperial Truck Hire) 9.

Punte: 1. Franco Bellardi 17; 2. Alan van Heerden 15; 3. Nando Sdevanin (Pickfords) en Antonio Fernandes (Sunripe Fruits) 12 elk; 5. Michael Thomson 10; 6. Paolo Ferreira (Sunripe Fruits) 9; 7. Craig Nash en Manuel Cunha 8 elk; 9. Tony Impey (SAUK–TV4) 7; 10. Johnny Koen 6.

Portuguese cyclists disciplined

CERES. — The controversy surrounding the use of illegal stimulants in cycling took a dramatic twist in the Rapport Tour yesterday when disciplinary action was taken against two Portuguese riders after tests taken at Mossel Bay on Tuesday proved positive.

The Portuguese riders from the Sunripe Fruits team Paolo Ferreira who was second overall before yesterday's stage from Worcester to Ceres, and his teammate Antonio Fernandes were fined 1 000 Swiss francs each, given a one-year suspended sentence and forfeit any prize money won during the stage from Oudtshoorn to Mossel Bay.

They also suffer a 10-minute penalty each, which kicks them right out of contention for a place in the individual and the team competition.

Urine samples sent to Bloemfontein after the stage revealed that there was an illegal amphetamine in their system according to the SA Cycling Federation delegate on the tour Brigadier Arno Combrink.

The Portuguese team was outraged at the result of the tests and their team manager Orlando Alves, threatened to withdraw from the tour and fly home to Johannesburg immediately.

"I feel such a fool for bringing the Portuguese team out here," said Alves, who was the South African contact for a Portuguese team in the tour.

"The two riders were obviously a scapegoat for getting back at the Portuguese. I can guarantee that this will be the last time the Portuguese team visits this country."

Mr Alves was referring to an incident earlier this year in which South African professional Robbie McIntosh was found guilty of using illegal amphetamines during the Tour of Portugal. McIntosh was given a suspended sentence.

In the race itself Alan van Heerden, leader of the Southern Sun Peugeot squad struck with a vengeance on the drama-packed day when he won the eighth stage of the cycling tour from Worcester to Ceres yesterday.

The victory shot the resilient professional to within striking distance of the individual points prize and his superb climbing in the wind-swept mountain passes earned him the blue jersey for the King of the Mountains. The man known as "The Van" also leapt up from sixth to second position overall after this stage.

And al though The Van got the accolade at the finish it was a stage which belonged to the tour leader, Mark Beneke, of VFP.

Yesterday he showed that he has courage galore as well when he took the bit between his teeth and attacked the field into the full force of the howling Southeaster,

and adulate the images that they had of these persons who were made out to be demi-gods. They don't want to hear the truth because once the lies that propped up their heroes were exposed it toppled their world of false heroes. Some say let it lie and forget about it, just as in the case with Armstrong and company. Some people's lives crumbled as their heroes' lives were exposed for what it really was – just a lot of hot air.

You can steal money from someone and one day he can be repayed by receiving the money back. However, if you steal an opportunity where someone could win a title or win a Tour or receive sponsorship endorsements to make a living from, that can never be given back. That is the significance of the grievance non-users have. A lost opportunity cannot be regained. Nevertheless, I have a God who restored these lost opportunities in the form of leading me to eventually break 13 more world records and win at world championship level 8 gold and 5 silver medals.

With the advantage of years that have passed since these incidents, the repercussions are evident. Several of the abusers suffer the consequences of ill physical and mental health and some have died as a result of it. It just was not worth sacrificing future health for false fame. Once a cyclist is caught positive his past and future performances will always be shrouded in a cloud of suspicion. Armstrong was asked in an interview if he could turn back the clock, would he again do what he did? He said yes, but possibly just better the next time around.

WAT PRAAT ONS ALLES?

Meer vrae as antwoorde ná Wimpie se skorsing

Posbus 692, Kaapstad.

ALLES lyk vir ons nie pluis met die skorsing van die Weermag-jaer Wimpie van der Merwe uit die Rapport-fietstoer nie, want dit het meer vrae laat ontstaan as waarop tot dusver antwoorde verstrek is. En antwoorde is noodsaaklik as die sport nie op die ou end die lydende party wil wees nie.

Van der Merwe is aanvanklik met R50 beboet omdat hy "'n verklaring aan die pers gedoen het." Waarom dit verkeerd is dat hy met enige persman gepraat het, is vir ons onduidelik, want sedert die begin van die toer is die dag se skofwenner 'n paar keer deur die SAUK-TV aan die woord gestel — ook ná die skorsing van Van der Merwe.

As 'n deelnemer dus nie met die pers mag praat nie, hoekom word die "verbod" nie omvattend gemaak sodat die swye ook op die SAUK-TV van toepassing is nie? Dit is mos dubbele maatstawwe.

En as dit gaan om *wat* Van der Merwe gesê het, is die boete en die skorsing ewe onverstaanbaar. Ons het die gewraakte berig wat tot die tugoptrede aanleiding gegee het, gelees en herlees, en tot die gevolgtrekking gekom dat daarin niks staan wat naastenby 'n boete of 'n skorsing kan regverdig nie.

● Vir eers het Van der Merwe, soos hy dit self later duidelik gestel het, nooit verklaar dat jaers in die huidige toer, wat môre hier in die Kaap eindig, verbode opkikkers gebruik het nie. En ten tweede het hy nooit enige spesifieke groep jaers — beroepsryers of amateurs — beskuldig nie.

LIGGERAAK

In die lig hiervan val dit dus vreemd op dat die beroepsjaers so erg ontstoke was oor wat gesê is dat hulle glad 'n spoedvergadering belê het, met 'n boikot gedreig en selfs ná die aanvanklike boete vir Van der Merwe geëis het dat hy verdere deelname ontsê word.

Die vernaamste antwoord wat vereis word, is op die vraag waarom die beroepsmanne so liggeraak is dat hulle só reageer sonder dat hulle as sg. sondaars uitgewys is. Ons insinueer nie daardeur dat hulle 'n skuldige gewete het nie, maar hul optrede kan dit so laat lyk.

Enige bewering deur die beroepsjaers dat hulle maar net hul sport se naam skoon wil hou, gaan net nie op nie. Hoekom was die amateurs dan nie ook ontsteld nie, of gee die beroepsmanne te kenne dat die amateurs nie ook omgee vir die sport waaraan hulle deelneem nie?

● Dit moet ook vir enigeen wat die belang van sport, insluitende fietsry, op die hart dra, verontrustend wees dat die toerbestuur vir alle praktiese doeleindes voor 'n magsblok geswig het toe Van der Merwe geskors is.

ONREG

Ons sal verbaas wees as dié afleiding nie ontken word nie, maar die toerbestuur het onses insiens gereageer op 'n koerantberig en geswig voor die druk van die beroepsjaers.

Dit is geen gesonde toedrag van sake nie. Die skade wat magsblokke kan aanrig, is reeds male sonder tal bewys op alle lewensterreine. Voorbeelde is oorbodig.

Van der Merwe is 'n onreg aangedoen wat moeilik reggestel kan word. 'n Amptelike verskoning van alle partye wat op een of ander manier deel gehad het aan sy skorsing, sal beslis nie onvanpas wees nie. Dit is die eerbare weg vir enigiemand wat regtig die sport wil dien.

LOUIS VAN WYK

Sport reveals character. It acts as an amplifier. What is already in you will just come out louder. A cheating sportsman operates with the same value system in business as what he operates within the sports arena. The principle of cheating, as long as you are not caught, is somehow accepted in sport, not only by the perpetrator but by the general public. Follow the social media debates of people trying to justify what Armstrong did. Because his peers were all doing the same the playing field was level, they say. The assumption is therefore that this behaviour is acceptable as long as or when all cheat. How does that sound in business or in a relationship?

I think I would be forgiven for being highly sceptical about the 'fame' of sportsmen, just as I am highly sceptical of the fame and influence of the created character that an actor portrays. Sport is show business as is acting, creating a persona, playing a role. Branding and creating a persona is the work of the public relations department of a sponsor or an agent and then to sell the persona. The media amplifies the persona because it sells newspapers or generates clicks. Eventually, we all fall for the falsehood. Fame and being well known does not guarantee a sound lifestyle or a sound character.

To neutralize this fake life of fame I live an authentic, transparent life. I am not trying to imitate the life of someone else or acting out a role. I don't compete with others. I attempt to be the best I can be irrespective of the competition. In the morning as I leave the world of dreams for the world of wakefulness, I remind myself that life is not a dress rehearsal. I live my dream daily. I try to live in such a way that I put a smile on God's face because I am fulfilling my purpose on earth. By living the life God called me for and surely that includes my cycling, I am fulfilled, I have no regrets and am content.

A further example of the injustices suffered and the abuse of power was in the 1986 Argus Cycle Tour. During this time, I was busy with my National Service. I formed part of their cycling team who was entered for the Argus Tour in Cape Town. I served my 3 months suspension imposed on me in the 1985 Rapport Tour. I could not race in any sanctioned event of the SACF up till 31 Dec '85.

The cycling politics of the time was very strained and polarised. The Argus Tour (ACT) was a Western Province Pedal Power Association (WPPPA) initiative and SACF registered cyclists were banned by the SACF to participate in it. Pedal Power and the SACF were not in the same camp. In 1986 things changed. The Pedal Power was making overtures to the SACF to allow their riders to participate in their events. This relationship was very fragile and conditional. A registered section was created in the Tour. The ACT made use of SACF officials to officiate because there was an official SACF category. The bettering of this relationship eventually led to the ACT becoming a UCI sanctioned event and increasing in international stature.

The only way we could participate in the past was by not registering with the SACF until after the ACT in April. The ACT introduced the beginning of the road season. We thus had to sacrifice competing in the last part of the track season from 1 Jan till after the ACT to be able to participate in the event, which was the highlight of the year for many cyclists. We called it the world championship for fun riders. I decided not to register with the SACF until after the

Argus Tour. It opened up more categories to win: fastest time and first non-registered rider.

I was seeded to start in group D as a non-registered rider, 15 minutes after group A, the licensed SACF riders. Fellow teammate, Lourens Smith, the eventual winner of the 1989 Rapport Tour, and I were both seeded in D and worked ourselves through the groups, chasing the front riders. At Small Chappies, about three quarters into the 105 km race, we received a time check. We have gained 12 of the 15 minutes on the front group. By then Lourens was dropped and I was the only one chasing but was losing time that I gained as the race heated up at the front.

The race finished in Camps Bay. The system was that your time was taken as you cross the line and your time was then posted in the form of a computer printout on notice boards about every 15-30 minutes. You could view your time or wait for the Argus newspaper to get the same information.

The winner of the ACT changed ownership a short while after the finishing sprint. The race referee disqualified both Alan van Heerden, who won the sprint and Jonathan Heard, for infringements on the course. The race was awarded to Ertjies Bezuidenhout. I crossed the line some minutes after them but in a faster overall time of 2:40, just more than half a minute faster than Bezuidenhout.

Whilst waiting for my official time to be posted I was approached by Lawrence Whittaker, chairman of Pedal Power and informed that I was disqualified from the race. No reasons were given.

By now I was quite desensitised by actions like these as petty politics were not my cup of tea. I just let it be. However, I was later in the year invited to compete in the Good Hope 100 Team Triathlon in Cape Town (in Oct 86). At the pre-function dinner, I was approached by a gentleman from Rotary. I believe he said he was the chairman. He introduced himself and said he wanted to make use of the opportunity to apologize to me for what happened at the '86 ACT. I was shocked to hear the story behind my disqualification.

Since I was persona non grata to the SACF and them realising that their arch-enemy had set the fastest time for the ACT they requested Pedal Power to disqualify me. The reason given to WPPPA was that I was a suspended rider and could not have entered and participated in the event, though my suspension was only till 31 December '85. Pedal Power and Rotary did not want to make a fuss and protest the unfairness as they were trying to establish a relationship with the government recognised cycling body. By offering me as the sacrificial lamb to the SACF they prevented a showdown. Relations improved dramatically from there onwards.

The scrubbing of evidence of me competing in the '86 ACT was so thorough that even the entries of Lourens Smith and I were removed as if we never participated in that ACT edition. Whether this was on purpose or through sloppiness I could not yet determine.

When looking at the life of the Biblical Joseph who was sold into slavery, being wrongly accused and jailed innocently he always enjoyed God's favour. The Dreams and the WHY of his life that God gave him as a young man kept him focused. Eventually his gifting to interpret dreams and the continuous favour of God made way for him into the king's palace. When he was eventually elevated to the second most powerful man in Egypt he did not use that as licence to take retribution on those who caused him injury but saw the bigger picture God had, to eventually benefit Israel, his family. God was accompanying all along.

The unjust treatment of the SACF and cycling officials could not deativate God's favour in my life and their actions had unintended consequences of nudging me towards all my world championship titles and world records, something they had no control over and could not deny me. Had my expulsion from SA cycling not occurred in 1987 I would possibly just have competed locally and not have moved on to greater challenges internationally. Without these accomplishments there would have been no influence. With no influence there would have been no platform and no testimony as I have today.

THE INFLUENCERS

A person who left fingerprints of significance on my life is my pastor, Allan Bagg. He has been the shepherd for our family since 1998. God knows who you need when He places a man of God in your life. In my case, He placed someone with a strong gift of teaching and someone who understands how faith works. Through him, the power of God became active in my life and not just the knowledge of God. The activation of faith and understanding the power of the faith-filled spoken Word is the legacy he leaves in my life.

Several prophecies have been made over my life and my family. When a true prophetic person makes these utterances, I pay attention and warfare with them. I regularly remind

Allan & Janine Bagg with the Van der Merwes.

God and Satan. I remind God about his promises and I warn Satan with them. There are particularly two prophets who prophesied and whose prophecies are coming to pass. It will be worthwhile sharing these encounters.

After a couple of weeks of fasting, God gave me on 23 Dec 2001 Isaiah 58: 12 as a prophecy for me and my family. Paraphrased it is –

> *Your family will deliver to the Lord what past generations have let disintegrate. You will reclaim what the enemy has claimed and restore generations to the Lord. You will be called the healer of God's wrath and the one who restores hope.*

On 23 Oct 2002, whilst attending our home cell group our hostess invited someone in a prophetic ministry to minister to us that evening, Josef Oosthuizen. As he walked into the living room, he pointed his finger directly at me and said, 'I want to speak to that rich person tonight'. I was offended. At that point in our life, we were financial down and out, for nearly a year already without an income and I thought the hostess briefed him before the meeting to please encourage this person who is financially in dire straits. He prophesied to each individual and when it was my turn, I told him to please say nothing except what the Lord tells him and not what he has been briefed on by the hostess. He was taken aback and told me that he has not seen the hostess, in three months, since this meeting. I was satisfied that he was not going to be my hostess' ventriloquist.

He started prophesying and we recorded it to write it down later. He prophesied about my future businesses, one which became a reality exactly 2 years later and which has been my main business ever since. This was less than 5 minutes that impacted my life irrevocably. This was the rocket booster firing, not a nudging. This did not only have a directional impact, but it caused acceleration.

Josef Oosthuizen

Ed Traut, a prophet of God, ministered to me several times over a couple of years and spoke words over me that I could warfare with, in life and death situations. He was the person who prophesied that God has placed years to my life, that I shall become an old man and always be healthy. This assured me that I can choose life because it has been promised to me. His nudgings constantly kept me on course. He prophesied our financial breakthrough just before it happened.

I take the prophetic seriously and when these men of God touch me, I don't just desire their fingerprints, but their handprints! They are instruments to confirm what I hear from the

Holy Spirit. Ultimately God touches our lives through people. The fingerprints of people, good and bad are allowed by God. This way the pot is formed. We decide whether the pot is for holy or worldly use.

God has the sole right to use my life and all He added to it as a tool and a platform for whatever purpose He wants. Whatever I am I am by grace and whatever I achieved I achieved by grace. He allowed things to happen in my life, good and bad, to encounter people good and evil, to form me. He let it all work out for the good in the end.

Ed Traut

What happens in this life will have intended and unintended consequences when I am not here anymore. The legacy eventually lies in whether my life experiences were nudgings and whether my life's fingerprints had an effect of helping others reach their Godly destination, accomplishing what they were set here for. We are all interconnected, playing a part in the master plan of God's cosmic design.

I ask myself; will they one day say that my life had the same consequences too, just as the width of a Roman horse's butt had on the design of the Space Shuttle's rocket booster?

www.ingramcontent.com/pod-product-compliance
Lightning Source LLC
Chambersburg PA
CBHW080225170426
43192CB00015B/2749